Encore!

Encore!

A BOOMER'S GUIDE TO ROCKING YOUR RETIREMENT

MARILYN MYRICK WATSON

Encore! A Boomer's Guide to Rocking Your Retirement
Published by Bird Mountain Press
Littleton, CO

ISBN: 978-1-7329100-0-3

SELF-HELP / Personal growth / Happiness

QUANTITY PURCHASES: Schools, companies, professional groups, clubs, and other organizations may qualify for special terms when ordering quantities of this title. For information, email marilynmwat@gmail.com.

This book is printed in the United States of America.

Dedicated to my biggest fans
(or they won't be in The Will)

Ladd, Teal, Sage, and Luke

"It's time to start living the life you've imagined."

– Henry James, American Author 1843–1916

Table of Contents

Encore: the call from the audience for a repeat or additional performance.

Rock: if a person rocks, he or she is cool or awesome!

You rock: used to describe someone who is cool or awesome.

To rock something: to do it well and with confidence.

Rock star: anyone in a field or profession that is highly admired: a master of his or her domain.

Foreword

Congratulations to you! First for retiring or beginning to think about your retirement; what an exciting time! Second, for picking up *this* book. Many books about retirement focus on the financial aspect of retirement, investments, and how to make your money last as long as you do. Those things are important. And, so is rocking your life and your retirement. That's exactly what *Encore! A Boomer's Guide to Rocking Your Retirement* does. With a 360-degree look at all that retirement is, *Encore!* guides you in making your upcoming years fun, vibrant and rewarding. After all, if you're going to retire, why not rock it?

My name is Kristi Staab and I am the owner and Chief Rock Star of Kristi Staab Enterprises, LLC, and the founder of Lead Like a Rock Star™. We help individuals, groups and teams reach the pinnacle of success. That's what Encore will do for you-help you create a successful rock star retirement.

How you play your *Encore!* in the year ahead depends on attitude, being, and choice. You might be thinking, "Hey, I'm retiring, I'm not looking to perform at the highest level anymore; I want to relax." Absolutely you do and you deserve to do just that. With a positive attitude and making conscious choices about your health and fitness, your way of giving back, sharing life with your grandchildren and more, you will have a full, rich life AND time to relax and enjoy the sunset. This book guides you to do that and more. You will learn to use your dreams to plan for and create the retirement you want. That is what Marilyn Watson wants for you. This book gives you the "how to" create your new lifestyle, not fall into one.

In 2010, Marilyn and I met at the Apple Store. We were each there working on our presentations for our new businesses. Her intelligent yet light-hearted personality was apparent immediately. Fortunately for you as a reader, her personality shines through in this book, making your reading and journey both informative and fun.

The world and your family have benefitted by all you have done in the years leading up to this moment. Why stop making the world a better place now? We greatly need people of character, values, and ideals to pass on those traits to the rest of us; making your life a legacy that lasts for future generations. Do it like a rock star!

- Kristi Staab, MBA, is driven by her passion to guide people from around the globe and see them transform into strong, impactful, positive, and influential leaders. Chief Rock Star Kristi Staab shares her innovative, inspiring, and influential Lead Like a Rock Star™ approach to discover, hone and put into action, your rock star leader within.

Introduction

There's a movement afoot! Baby boomers are the originators of movements, right? We protested the Việt Nam War, banned the bomb, burned the bras! What baby boomer doesn't like a good movement? (Ok, I should re-phrase that.) What baby boomer doesn't want to start a revolution? We are going to rename, reclaim, and recreate what it means to be retired!

We are living longer, and thus, retirement doesn't mean what it used to. Back in the 50s, those who retired were worn out and ready to sit in their rockers and enjoy the sunshine, as they had only about ten to fifteen years left in their lives. In 2020 and beyond, people will live twenty—sometimes thirty—good, productive years past retirement. We have the opportunity to use our wisdom, energy, and expertise to contribute to society. We were the Peace Corps generation; we wanted to help people around the world, to sow the seeds of peace. Somehow, we grew up, fell in love, raised families, and didn't get to continue our twenty-something dreams. Now, with retirement upon us, we can!

There are now groups seeking to join forces and really create something new in terms of retirement. Some even want to change the name altogether. Encore, out of Grand Rapids, shares stories of retirees making a difference. Jane Pauley and AARP created Life Reimagined and want to hear about your dreams and the differences you are making. You do not have to join a movement officially in order to rock your retirement. Together, we will explore ways for you to have a retirement that meets all your goals and dreams.

This book is not about financial planning, Medicare, or taxes in retirement. I hope that by the time you are looking at this book, you've had your financial plan in place for a decade or more. And, trust me, you don't want me to do your investing for you. I had a relatively large sum of money and invested in swamp land in Florida. (Actually, it was to be a housing community in California.) Somehow, the investing partner went default, and my money went far away; I never did quite understand what happened there. So, I'll leave the financial planning to the experts.

If you are looking for advice in those three areas, please consult a financial planner or your accountant. For other information, there are abundant resources in your local library, the book stores, or online. Three that you may like are:

Medicare information: www.medicare.gov

Taxes: www.incometax.gov

Financial planning: www.forbes.com/.../
the-1-page-financial-plan

Allow me to introduce my brother, Ralph. He is twelve years older than I am. He has dementia and stopped driving a car two years ago. He doesn't know where I live and has to take a nap after his morning outing. Every ten minutes he asks, "When does your train leave?"

His retirement from the Indiana steel mills was a short-lived one. He came home, picked up the paper, watched TV, and drove his wife to and from work. For some, that is just fine. For me—not on your life! I want more. My knees still work and I want to ski, travel, volunteer, hike, and walk my dog. I plan to laugh and serve my community. I have productive years ahead—and so do you. Let's not waste them. In

Encore!, we will explore ways to help you do just that. Let's start with your last day at work.

The whistle blows, the bell rings, and you are ready to pick up your last paycheck. Congratulations! Now what? Are you going home to sit in your rocker on the front porch? Are you going to turn on the TV and see what interests you? Do you have a plan, or are you just going to let life happen to you?

It's natural to have questions and concerns about this upcoming chapter in your life. After all, as kids, we played Fireman, Cowboy, Mom, or Teacher. I bet you never said, "Let's pretend we're retired!" or "Let's pretend we're Grandpa." Retirement, for most of us, is unchartered waters.

When I attended the mandatory preretirement seminar in my school district, the director of Human Resources asked, "Who has something lined up for after retirement?" Many hands went up. "Good," he said, "you are ready for retirement; the rest of you are not."

Nothing is in stone here in this next chapter of your life. Give yourself the grace to grow into the person or lifestyle you want for the next twenty to twenty-five years. However, don't wait too long. There are things you need to do soon in order to make this a great time of your life, and that's what you'll discover in this book. If you want to live the rest of your life with meaning and intentionality, let's talk!

As a child before school, your life was dictated by your parents. In school, you did what the teachers told you to do (most of the time). Then, with that long-awaited job, your boss was in charge. Now it's your time, and YOU get to make the life you want: a life created around your interests, your desires, your purpose. We each have specific gifts that were bestowed upon us, and we have only one life to live. This isn't a dress rehearsal! In retirement, we've been given another opportunity to accept who we are and keep on keeping on or take a leap of faith and try something new. Let's make the most of the life we've been given.

In my first counseling class in grad school, the professor said there were five areas in a healthy well-balanced life: personal growth, wellness, spirituality, relationships, and work.

We go through different stages of life, and in those stages more time is spent in some of these areas than others. As a kid, play was paramount: work and spirituality, not so much. In our twenties, thirties, and forties, work was the most important thing. Now, it's time to play again. But is that all you want to do—play? I think it's important to keep learning, to keep having relationships, and (perhaps for the first time) develop your spiritual self. This is the time many of us stop accumulating and begin giving and sharing what we have learned with others.

> "If a man, for whatever reason, has the opportunity to lead an extraordinary life, he has no right to keep it to himself."
> - Jacques Eves Cousteau

To live your life to the fullest, let's look at these five areas.

1. Personal Growth

Keep your mind open to learning new things and keep the mind sharp. Our grandparents did crossword puzzles, right? We can write on our laptops, learn a language, take classes. It's important to keep learning!

2. Wellness

Without a healthy body, this retirement gig is going to be short—or painful. The goal here is to be able to enjoy the life you have in your younger retirement years and prolong a good, healthy, active life. Exercise and good nutrition are of paramount importance.

3. Spirituality

This is your relationship with God or The Universe or a higher purpose—whatever gives meaning to your life. The fact that it gives meaning to your life makes it the most important of all five areas. That doesn't mean you should focus only on developing your spirituality. Even if your spirituality is strong, you won't live life to the fullest without activity in the other areas.

4. Relationships

You know the saying: no one on their deathbed says, "I wish I'd spent more time at work." Investing in personal relationships will play an important role in the overall health of your retirement. The relationships we have with our family, friends, and community are those that enrich our lives.

5. Work

Yes, you have worked all your life, and now you are retiring. Why talk about work? We will talk about it because it's true that "all work and no play makes Jack a dull boy." But the opposite is also true. At this point in your life, work can be where you volunteer or time spent with grandchildren or a new hobby or some kind of paid work—either in your former career or in a new area. I will be talking about the types of things that you can do as a retiree to make your life both fun and meaningful. Work can also help us make a little extra money or give us the insurance coverage we might need, and that's meaningful too!

In this book, we'll talk about these five areas previously mentioned, as well as some additional ideas that help make the most of retirement. I will introduce you to a few of the many retired men and women I have interviewed. They have stories to tell about what they *thought* would happen in retirement and what actually *did* happen. Sometimes it was the same thing, sometimes it was a surprise, and in some cases, it was a lesson learned. Whichever it was, their stories may inspire or enlighten you, or simply make you smile. We will look at fitness, food, volunteer opportunities, travel, work, and money-saving tricks (and who doesn't like that?) We will explore spirituality. We'll look at being single, or reimagining a long marriage or friendship.

It is *your* time now, and only you can create your rockin' retirement. Let's jump to the end: What do you want to look back on in twenty, twenty-five years? Do you want to see a happy, fulfilled retirement in which you contributed something to someone? Do you want to see yourself trying new things, going to new places? Or are you happy to see yourself sitting and fishing for twenty years? Whatever you choose is right for you! But what you choose requires thought and preparation, so please read on!

This encore is your golden opportunity for YOU to create the life you want with the means you have at hand. Let's rock this!

1
Your Story
So Far

"All the world's a stage," William Shakespeare said, and thus, we are all in a play. If this is true, we are definitely in the Third Act. In fact, we have been given an encore! We have done a good job so far and have time for more. So, here we have a remarkable opportunity to write our own ending. I like to think I'm not a control freak, but I get real excited about the chance to determine what happens in the next part of my life. I can design it and, God willing, live it out my way. But first, we need to know the backstory. To help recreate this, I've included exercises for you to do. To get the most out of what I'm sharing, please complete them. It's not challenging, and the rewards will be greater if you do.

Please get a piece of printer or notebook paper, lay it horizontally, and draw a line across the middle.

Starting at the left side, mark in the significant moments in your life: moments that marked a different direction than where you thought you were going, significant turning points in your life. We are making your life story on a timeline. Using a scale of one to ten, draw a line up or down from your center line and give those moments a value. Lines up reflect positive experiences; lines down are for the negatives. For example, on my personal timeline, I had the fact that I was a rooster in my first grade play as significant but only gave it a four in value. (It was important to me because from that point on, I knew I was comfortable on stage and wanted to continue acting on one.)

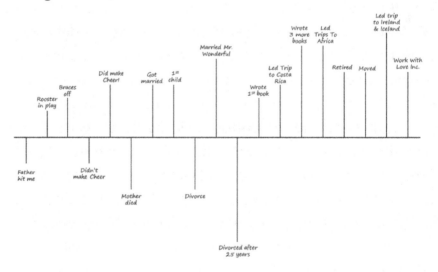

When you are finished, take a look at your ups and downs and realize that you survived all the storms and came up stronger on the other side. I was teaching a class recently and had folded back the part of my timeline after my divorce at the age of fifty-seven. That was probably the lowest point in my life, even lower than my mother's death from suicide. But, when I unfolded the paper from that point forward, everything was on the plus side of the line! I had come from a devastating time in my life, and *everything* I did afterwards was positive. I wrote five books. I led trips to Africa, Peru, the Galapagos Islands, Switzerland, Iceland, Ireland, and Scotland. I moved to a new city and am surrounded by all four of my children and all nine of my grandchildren. I developed and teach a class for Love INC, helping people out of poverty. Wow! It was shocking to see this in such a dramatic fashion. Doing this exercise helps you see how strong you are or prompts you to see that you had better get busy and put things in your life that are meaningful to you.

Next, look at the roles you play in your life: you are a mother, daughter, friend, volunteer, golfer, mentor, friend. You can list them here:

FIVE ROLES

_____

_____

_____

_____

_____

Then list two or three goals you have for yourself in each of these roles.

Role-Mother
    Goal-to be the kind of mother who creates memories
    Goal-to keep the photo books up-to-date
    Goal-to give the children to give my adult children space and grace to be their own persons.

Role-Golfer
    Goal-to break 100
    Goal-to spend at least twenty minutes a week on short game practice
    Goal-to play twice a month in summer.

List some of your goals here:
Role One: _____ (parent, husband, golfer—it's your choice)
    Goal One: _____
    Goal Two: _____
    Goal Three: _____

Role Two: _____
    Goal One: _____
    Goal Two: _____
    Goal Three: _____

Role Three: _____
    Goal One: _____

Goal Two: _____

Goal Three: _____

Role Four: _____

    Goal One: _____

    Goal Two: _____

    Goal Three: _____

Role Five: _____

    Goal One: _____

    Goal Two: _____

    Goal Three: _____

These goals you have will help you live intentionally in the upcoming years. For me, I saw areas in which I wanted to make sure I was growing and improving. Especially golf. I had told my aunt I would save golf until I retired. She wisely said, "No! You have to learn now while you are young, so you can enjoy it when you retire."

Finally, imagine yourself in these roles, one at a time, and pretend it's the final scene of a movie. Imagine the image: you as a mother with your children, the sun is setting, the music is playing, and the credits are rolling. What do you see? You in the kitchen making cookies for the grand-children? You climbing Kilimanjaro with your son?

> "Twenty years from now, you will be more disappointed by the things you didn't do than by the ones you did do. So throw off the bowlines, sail away from the safe harbor. Catch the trade winds in your sails. Explore. Dream. Discover."
> – Mark Twain

In my scene as a mother, I vividly saw my four children at my funeral. Oddly, the four siblings were in the front row, and their spouses were in the row behind them. Each of my darlings had a different memory of me. One saw me on the handlebars of his bike, riding along the beach in California. Another saw me swimming with stingrays, and a third child saw me rafting the Colorado River. My youngest son saw me with him, soaring in a parasail over the ocean in Mexico.

What this showed me was that none of them thought, "Our mother was so sweet; she was always baking cookies." No! My kids saw me as an active mother who was always looking for more experiences. This has shaped what I do with my adult children even now; I look for experiences to share with them, rather than just having them over for Sunday dinner. (Besides, they think I can't cook—works for me!) For Christmas, I have asked the grown children not to get me "things" as gifts. Instead, I ask for time and shared experiences with them. One son gave me tickets to a basketball game for just the two of us. Another is taking me on a fishing trip and a third, an iPhone-led scavenger hunt in downtown Denver with the family and two teenagers. That should be fun!

Finally, please get another sheet of paper, and again lay it horizontally. Then mark off from zero to 100 by tens. Next, put a mark by where you are today and another by where you think you'll leave this planet.

```
0  10  20  30  40  50  60  70  80  90  100
_____X_____ X_____
```

Next, tear the paper where you are now, where you marked the first "x." Then tear it again where you think the end will be, where you put the second "x." Hold up what you have left up. *That* is what you have to work with in creating the retirement of your dreams. *That* is what you have to work with to make a difference in your family and in the world.

That's not a lot of time left, is it? This gives a clear picture why one needs to get it done now!

What's left

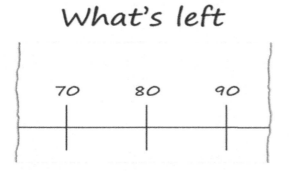

DO THE WORK; do the exercises mentioned in this chapter. You can use the spaces provided or use your own paper, but I promise, you will have some interesting revelations. What you learn from this will help you as you go forward with your retirement planning.

This is how we can create the retirement that we want, in order to have a powerful encore. We can live it our way; we are creating the ending to our own story, not passively going through each day waiting to see what happens to us.

2
Transition Into Retirement

It is no wonder that people are seeking a new term other than "retirement" to describe this time of life. We are not retiring in the sense of sitting back or fading into the woodwork. People who retire now are healthy, robust, and have plans for today and tomorrow.

Richard N. Bolles developed the three boxes of life theory, which illustrated retirement in our parents' and grandparents' age.

This concept originally included education, work, and retirement as the three progressions of life.

Education	Work	Retirement

As longevity increased, the retirement box took on the term "leisure."

Education	Work	Leisure

After more time the three stages, went to four stages.

Development	Productivity	Development Productivity Leisure	Leisure

Peter Laslett, a historian from Cambridge University, realized that the old idea of retirement was just not appropriate in the current days. People were more robust and the formerly rigid stages could be occurring in various ages. "He developed a much more fluid representation of retirement, shown in the illustration as more of a 'summit' rather than a boxed view of life."

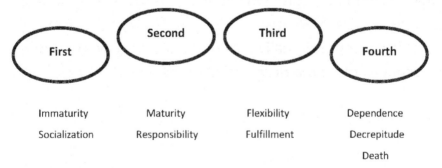

First	Second	Third	Fourth
Immaturity	Maturity	Flexibility	Dependence
Socialization	Responsibility	Fulfillment	Decrepitude
			Death

In whatever way you look at it, retirement can be a shock to your system. You have left that career by which you have been identified. You are no longer a janitor, a nurse, a bus driver, a teacher, an accountant. You are—what?

A retired news editor told me it felt like he had post-traumatic stress disorder when his career ended; not all PTSD events come from battlefield experiences. PTSD can also come after a shock, death, or sudden loss. Certainly when forty to fifty years of working come to an end, and if you don't have an immediate plan for what comes next, a person can lose a degree of psychological balance. It certainly happened to this former editor; here's his story.

James the editor

James had been involved with newspapers his entire life. As an editor he said, "It was a privilege to have a front-row seat to the first rough drafts of history in small towns, great cities, the nation's capital, and elsewhere in the world. But with that life came constraints. Journalists are discouraged from taking sides, joining causes, or talking about their party affiliations.

The "objective me" endured. The publications and websites I worked for reached millions over the years. But the "subjective me" longed to be heard about matters I cared deeply about. Working for newspapers, having editorial page positions that did not align with my core, contributed to a lack of fulfillment at the end of my career. Between my inner voice wanting to be heard and the painful process of laying off people I had hired twenty-five years before, the call to freedom came more often to my ears and heart."

James had a job at a large Midwest newspaper for his last position. His name was in brass on the door-plate, and he answered everyone's questions about content, subject, and deadlines. At his big retirement party, he was roasted and toasted for all his years in the business. It was a satisfying end to his long and successful career. However, it turned out he needed to go back to the building the next day. People nodded to him, but no one stopped and said hello. No one asked for his opinion. Several people would not make eye contact. He went down the hall to his office to discover it was no longer his! His nameplate was gone and the new guy was in. "Just like that, my life as I knew it was over," James said. He and his wife moved to the warm, sunny Southeast, where they had previously spent some time. It took six months of decompression and enjoying their leisure before he and his wife felt centered and knew what they wanted to do for their encore.

What does James' story tell us? Sometimes retirement is not easy. It isn't all parties, vacations, and having no care in the world. It truly can resemble PTSD. Questions such as, "Where am I? Who am I? Who needs me? Anyone?" can fill your mind. If they do, take a deep breath and get back to that place of grace. Allow yourself to go with the flow, to take the time to discover your life in its new role.

As a way of reducing the shock of the hard stop, many companies across the nation are letting employees choose a shortened workweek of three or four days once they get close to retiring. Dr. Ken Dychtwald, a psychologist who founded Age Wave, says that gradually shortening that workweek makes the transition "kind of a glide path instead of a hard stop." With a new mindset from companies on how to treat retirees, the PTSD effect can be greatly reduced.

"Consider retirement as a period of trial and error. You may not get it right on your first try," Dychtwald says. You have time to try out different activities, different social activities, different ways to organize your day. "There's a whole world of opportunities sitting in front of you, and now you have the time to poke around," he says. "What is particularly traumatic is thinking that everything is final, and all your decisions are permanent. They need not be. Consider that you are retiring 'to' something, not 'from something.'"

Whether you retire suddenly or gradually, you may expect a time of disorientation—the "crazies." We do not talk about that confusion in our lives at any time. You know, when people ask us, "How are you?" we really don't say, "I'm going crazy; I can't sleep. I don't know whether I should retire, refire, or take a nap." Expect that to occur and take a deep breath and continue making plans and trying new things. Some say ninety days is a good amount of time to assess what you are doing and feeling. You already know your core values and what brings you joy. As you plan this encore in your life, be aware of including experiences that you value, as well as experiences just for fun. Make sure you are taking care of yourself with exercise and stress relief at this time too.

Many teachers choose to go on a vacation at the time when the new school year begins—the first one in which they are not back preparing their classrooms. After five years of retirement, I still have back-to-school dreams every August. Really, five years later and those little darlings and chalkboards and lesson plans still come back to haunt me.

As for my new identity, how I think of myself is, "I am an explorer—a traveler. I'm on a journey of service and discovery." Reframe your thinking into "this is not the ending, it's a new beginning."

When you retire, there can be many different emotions that swirl around you: excitement, fear, dread, boredom, joy, confusion. Did you ever think, jealousy? Read about Spencer and Margaret, and see how that came into their story.

Some of us work at jobs that pay the rent. Some of us work at jobs or careers that we like. Some of us are fortunate enough to have passions that enable us to make a living from them. Meet Spencer and Margaret Lucas.

Spencer and Margaret, both musicians, have spent the past forty years or more teaching and performing. Spencer, a choral conductor, recently retired from a community chorus that he had conducted for the past forty-three years. Shortly before his retirement as a conductor, he retired from his full-time teaching position at a local community college.

Margaret, soprano and voice teacher, had retired from full-time teaching in her private studio, but continues to teach students from the community college, as well as producing an ongoing musical series dedicated to the solo voice.

Turning seventy, Spencer felt it was time to retire. Leaving not only the creative and conducting part of the chorus, he left the people with whom he had deep relationships over the years. If he had stayed in town when the new conductor took over, it might have felt like watching your ex-wife fall in love with a younger man. It was an emotionally difficult time for him.

To make the transition easier, the morning after they were celebrated at the retirement party, the Lucases left town. The first stop was New York City, where their daughter received the prestigious Avery Fisher Award. She became the first flutist to receive the Fisher Prize, which is awarded every few years to recognize musical excellence, vision, and leadership. What a way to crown a lifetime career in music—watching your daughter gain recognition for her accomplishments so early in her career!

After another emotional day, they left the country for Rome, Italy. What a wonderful place to restore and refresh their musical souls. They traveled the country, saw operas, and enjoyed the Italian culture. They had no concrete plans other than waking each day to enjoy unscheduled time and this new cultural adventure. For the first time in many years, neither of them had tangible commitments or schedules in their lives.

Spencer had given himself the gift of grace: a loving, carefree time to adjust to leaving his beloved choral group in the capable hands of another maestro.

LIVE BY GRACE, NOT PERFECTION

In the religious world, grace is an enigmatic concept. Grace is good, grace is a gift, grace is not earned, and it can't be taken away. It just is. You can't control grace, you receive it, like the gift of a sunset that knocks your socks off. Like a concerto that moves you to tears. Like the thrill of a baby looking at you, crinkling his eyes in joy. Like the warm embrace of your loved one after your anger. Grace, it just is. In this time of transition, give yourself the gift of grace, allow yourself to experience many different things. Feel the anguish that comes with the loss of identity. Feel the freedom that comes with the loss of expectations. Go sailing, go golfing, go take a nap! Look at old photo albums and see what you used to love, see if that passion is still there. Now is the time to continue with the life you have, add new things, or create you all over again! But be careful because here's the thing about time: It only comes once. It is fleeting. When it's gone, it's gone. Use this time as the great gift it is.

> Grace is good,
> grace is a gift.
> Grace can't be earned,
> and it can't
> be taken away.
> It just is.

COME UP WITH A SCHEDULE

Many people have heard the advice, "Don't jump into everything right away; give yourself time to adjust to your new life." For some, that is too loose; they need some kind of plan. If that's you, then plan your daily life; come up with a structure: breakfast, walk, gym class, lunch with friends, midday bowling league. Don't retire and then just sit down and wait for what happens.

Look at these statistics from the A.C. Nielson Company:

- The average American watches four hours of TV a day.
- The average person spends an accumulation of NINE years in front of the TV.
- The average retiree watches forty-eight hours of TV a week or 104 full days a year.
- If a retiree starts at sixty-five and lives twenty more years, that is 2,080 DAYS of retirement in front of the TV.

So, let's not let that happen! 104 days a year of TV watching? Not for me. Let's make those schedules and plan those trips.

Sample Schedules
Joe

8 a.m. up, breakfast, news

9 a.m. gym

10:30 a.m. coffee with friends

12 p.m. lunch

1 p.m. nap (yes, they are allowed)

2–5 p.m. golf, bowling

6 p.m. dinner

7 p.m. woodworking in garage

8 p.m. read

9 p.m. TV

10 p.m. bed

Carrie

6 a.m up, coffee, meditation

7 a.m. breakfast

9 a.m. Zumba

10 a.m. home, shower, change

12 p.m. food bank work

1 p.m. lunch with friends

2:30 p.m. nap

3:30 p.m. walk the dog

4:30 p.m. fix dinner

5:30 p.m. eat

7 p.m. book club, couples bridge, etc.

10 p.m. bed

Marilyn's Weekly Schedule

Monday: Workout, lunches for homeless, visit family, writing time, dinner, tap lesson

Tuesday: Workout, Lifetime Learning class, writing, dinner, Toastmasters

Wednesday: Watch grandchildren, networking, dinner, Beer and Hymns

Thursday: Workout, lunch, ladies' bowling group, writing, class for low-income clients

Friday: Hike, midday book club, visit with friends, happy hour

Saturday and Sunday: Schedule varies

BEGIN YOUR RETIREMENT GRADUALLY

Some companies allow you to cut back on work time for a gradual, phased-in retirement. Other companies invite retirees back at busy times, such as end of the fiscal year or tax season. You might consider consulting on an "as needed" basis to your company or freelance with others.

> "Be mindful of how you approach time. Watching the clock is not the same as watching the sun rise."
> – Sophia Bedford-Pierce

Whether your company allows that or not, start thinking of retirement a year or two before you stop working cold turkey. If there is not a phase-out opportunity, here are some things you can try to prepare for retirement.

- Think of vacations prior to retirement as a trial run.
- Take longer vacations and leave the laptop at home. Don't do any work!
- Begin to look into recreational and volunteer opportunities that interest you.
- See what it feels like to spend a longer amount of time in the same house as your spouse. How will you handle that?

MAKE A LIST OF POSSIBILITIES

Talk to your friends and family, and ask what they envision you doing.

Some ideas could be in the field in which you currently work; others might be something entirely new that interests you. Make a list of the things you've always wanted to do, and see which fit with your life and finances now.

Rename this time "a new beginning"; don't think of it as an ending. And remember, this is a time of trial and error; nothing is in stone. If you don't work and are feeling totally unproductive and unfulfilled, try a part-time job. The opposite is also true. If you are working part-time and it feels like too much, leave it!

GETTING FOCUSED

Ask yourself the following questions, and use the blanks for your answers.

What I do now that I want to continue doing when I am retired (For example: bowling with the guys, woodshop.)

New things I want to do. (For example: take a photography class, learn Spanish, start a Thursday morning coffee meeting at IHOP.)

_____

_____

_____

_____

_____

_____

_____

Keep these lists and refer to them if you find yourself getting bored or "antsy."

Perhaps you can share these ideas with a friend who also recently retired. It's always good to have an accountability partner.

KEEP YOUR FRIENDS AND MAKE NEW ONES

It is important to have your friends around right now. As you develop a new identity and discover what is meaningful to you, it is important to stay connected. If you are finding yourself alone and isolated and can't seem to get motivated and are feeling depressed, talk to a pastor or counselor or someone who can help get the zest back in your living.

Retirement years are not a one-size-fits-all. Give yourself a period of adjustment and patience to see what works best for you. Realize that your lifestyle is open to change if and whenever you wish.

PREVIOUSLY IMPORTANT PEOPLE

Previously Important People (PIP), formerly VIPs, is a term used to identify people who previously commanded a great deal of attention and assistance but who must now get through an entire day on their own. (Just a bit of sarcasm here.) PIPS formerly had minions to make reservations, but now find themselves waiting on hold for the next available agent. I had a friend who, on his first Monday as a PIP, asked his wife to email him (she was in the next room). When she asked "Why, honey?" he answered, "I think my email is broken." He had been a high-powered lawyer in a large company on Friday. On Monday, he wondered why there were no emails in his inbox. Some things take a period of adjustment. A PIP, or anyone who has no hobbies that take up five hours a day, really has a lot of time to learn to fill.

HOBBIES YOU MIGHT LIKE

The Arts

Painting, musical instruments, theater and drama auditions, writing classes, cake decorating, photography, interior decorating, knitting, quilting, woodworking, jewelry making, pottery, poetry, memoir writing, or starting a band.

Outside

Bird watching, archery, canoeing, wildlife census, wildlife rescue, fly-fishing, deep sea fishing, tube fishing, astronomy, hiking, gardening, bonsai growing, dog training, hunting clubs, rifle clubs, antique car clubs and racing, or drone flying.

Inside

Genealogy, wine making, beer brewing, scrapbooking,

collectibles, renovating, billiards, boat making, barbecuing, culinary classes, dancing class, or vinyl record collecting.

Sports

Archery, badminton, tennis, swimming, boxing, bowling, karate, tai chi, cycling, croquet, motorcycle touring, horse riding, running, or track and field sports.

> "You know you're old when you're asked, 'Do you have hobbies?'"
> – Warren Beatty

This is just a tiny smattering of things you can do to add fun and activities to your daily routine. I'm sure you can find these or more that you will enjoy.

Robert Laura, writing in *Forbes Magazine*, states that some areas concern retirees more than others. One concern is feeling the groundhog effect, as in the movie in which Bill Murray had to relive every day the same way over and over. Without planning for activities, it just seems to be the same old thing, day after day.

Some people need more help and planning to break out of that cycle when retirement first starts. For many of us, using our parents' model of retirement is problematic. We are more vibrant, have more life left and, frankly, have greater need for mental stimulation, socialization, and achievement. Reach out to others, read articles, or get in touch with me if you find you are feeling stagnant and not enjoying the best retirement you can. You will find my contact information at the end of this book.

PRERETIREMENT QUESTIONS

1. Why do you want to retire?_____
   _____

2. Do you have a financial plan in place? _____
   _____

3. Do you know of ways to save money or live inexpensively? _____

4. Will you work part-time? _____

5. Do you have friends, or will you need to make new ones? _____

6. Do you have hobbies or ideas of what you want to do next? _____

7. Do you know where you will live? _____
   _____

8. Is your identity tied to your job, or can you make a new one? _____

9. Have you and your spouse or partner talked about retirement? _____

10. Do you and your partner agree on retirement issues?
    _____

11. Are you prepared for out-of-pocket health care costs?
    _____

The answers to these questions should be mostly "yes" to indicate that you have thought about and planned for a vibrant encore after your career comes to a close. If you have mostly negative answers, plan on spending some time researching or thinking about them. A family counselor or transition coach can be a great asset.

3
Big Mac
or Tofu

How's that fitness goal coming along? You know, the one where you were going to lose twenty pounds or be able to ride a bike in the Seniors Road Race. You don't have one? Well, it's time to make one!

If you have lived to sixty-five or seventy years of age and haven't done much to stay healthy, you had better start. Remember that even if you've had no health problems up until now, there is no guarantee you are getting out of here without any. We need to get checkups and live a balanced life. I'm not going to give you specifics other than "GO SEE YOUR DOCTOR NOW!" and get healthy—or this gift of retirement won't last long.

The cost of health care is a BIG concern to retiring individuals, and it should be. In May of 2017, CNN reported health care costs are bankrupting us. Studies show that a retired couple should expect to spend $240,000 on medical expenses after retirement. To add to that, women should expect to pay a little more, due to the fact that they typically outlive men. Where will that money come from? Your retirement savings! In order to rock this encore period, driving down the cost of health care is important to all of us. So, what can we do about it?

STAY HEALTHY. You and I both know what that means:

- Eat smartly
- Exercise regularly
- Skip the junk food we love so much

The good news is that it is never too late. Duke University research says that thirty minutes of moderate exercise four or five times a week can begin to reverse the negative effects of inactivity. The same is true of poor eating habits. In 1998, in the Journal of American Medicine Association, Dr. Dean Ornish said that eliminating poor eating habits by midlife and sustaining positive habits can add as many as fourteen years to one's life.

> "Running out of money pales in comparison to running out of family, friends, good health, and time."
> – Robert Laura

Some of us were not considered "athletes" in school. The choices were football, basketball, volleyball, and softball, and if those weren't sports we had skill in, well, we just didn't earn that big, gold letter. However, somewhere in our twenties, we tried running, tennis, or working out in a gym and discovered we were coordinated and could be considered athletes of sorts.

When you retire, and if you've stayed somewhat physically fit, there are many sports with designated age brackets (so we do have a chance to compete). Some of those sports are:

- Running
- Bowling
- Biking
- Senior rodeo
- Tennis
- Pickleball
- Racquet ball
- Track and field
- Swimming
- Horseshoes

The National Senior Games Association, a non-profit organization, is dedicated to motivating active adults to lead a healthy lifestyle through the Senior Games. National Senior Games had over 10,000 participants last year. A lot of these are track and field type, including discus, javelin, and shot put. These sports teams even travel around the country to compete. Consider this a fun lifestyle that mixes sports, friends, and traveling—all in one!

Check out www.seniorgames.org or National Senior Games Association at www.nsga.org

There's no doubt people today are staying active longer than previous generations, and the benefits of a healthful lifestyle are well-documented. In fact, at the end of 2014, the American College of Sports Medicine made the prediction that fitness programs for older adults would be one of the top ten fitness trends of the year ahead, and that certainly has come to pass.

> "My motto was always to keep swinging. Whether I was in a slump or feeling badly or having trouble off the field, the only thing to do was keep swinging."
> – Hank Aaron

On an individual (non-competitive) level, there are so many ways to keep the body moving. Consider walking, either with your precious pup or your wife or by yourself. Walking is a good way to meet some new people and share that awesome smile of yours and wish someone, "Good morning!" You'll both feel better.

Swimming is considered one of the best sports for those of us in this age bracket, as it does not put stress on the joints (no, not the rolled kind). Because being in water allows one to float, swimming is a great workout for people with osteoarthritis. According to Hirofumi Tanaka of the Cardiovascular Aging Research Lab, swimming reduces arterial stiffness in people with osteoarthritis. This can reduce the risk of heart-related problems. Because of the buoyancy factor, swimming is a great exercise for severely overweight people, as it is not as stressful as load-bearing exercise like running or other types of aerobic workouts. The recommended amount of time to be spent swimming as exercise is thirty minutes, three times a week. As in all sports, start slowly and take breaks until you are able to work up to that thirty-minute mark.

Because I live in a climate with cold winters, it limits the time I can swim outside, which is my preference. Joining a gym allows me to swim all year if I want.

SILVER SNEAKERS

Speaking of joining a gym, the Silver Sneakers Program is honored at many gyms and recreation centers, and you can work out for FREE! Their website says:

"MILLIONS ALREADY KNOW"

The Silver Sneakers program is aimed at keeping seniors healthy, active, and social. Many insurance programs cover this basic entry-level fitness program at participating gyms around the country. There are 13,000 gyms that do offer this free program to seniors who qualify. (Check your eligibility here: www.Silversneakers.com) The programs aim to empower boomers to defy the previous stereotypes and come at life with an "I can do it" attitude. Weights, treadmills, pools, and other amenities are included along with special classes and seminars in which you can learn new techniques or new sports. There is a Facebook page, Silver Sneakers, to give you a glimpse of what they have to offer.

The amenities are free, classes are free; let's do this!

Participating in sports and leagues is often a way to keep yourself committed to working out. If your intramural team is scheduled to play, you can't be home watching TV. Your local Parks and Recreation Center offers adult team sports from softball to adult ice hockey and one I'd like to try in Denver: curling. (I've never done it. I'm not Canadian; I might hate it, but it sure looks like fun.)

> "Men do not quit playing because they grow old; they grow old because they quit playing."
> – Oliver Wendell Holmes

One of the fastest growing sports, especially for seniors, is pickleball. It is a paddle sport created for all ages and skill levels. The rules are simple, and the game is easy for beginners to learn, but can develop into a quick, fast-paced, competitive game for experienced players.

Pickleball combines many elements of tennis, badminton, and ping-pong. It can be played both indoors or outdoors on a badminton-sized court and a slightly modified tennis net. It is played with a paddle and a plastic ball with holes like a whiffle ball and can be played as a singles or doubles game. Many Parks and Recreation facilities offer Pickleball "Boot Camps" to learn the sport. Take a look at your Parks and Rec mailer or online, and give it a try. I first learned in a church gym that offered lessons and rotation play as part of their health mission.

Skiing can still be enjoyed, and seniors are offered a reduced rate! I have seen many retired folks volunteer at ski resorts in the lodges and as mountain guides. These senior employees often find themselves living in the same lodges in the community and have a great social life—sounds like a win-win all the way around.

Yoga and group exercise classes are the best way for me to stay fit. I was a Jazzercise instructor in my early thirties, and I still go three or four times a week. Jazzercise is no longer like it was in the '80s, just for women wearing shiny tights and leg warmers, but it still has fun, upbeat music. That's good for two things: the music is fun to work out to, and it helps me look cool in the eyes of my grandkids when I can sing their songs! I love the popular music and the fun instructors and find that every now and then I still get up on stage. Whether it's Zumba or Jazzercise or something else, it is easy to modify to suit your fitness ability. What works for me is the accountability factor: Class starts at 9:30, and if I don't show up, friends call to see what's happening. I am a social person, so this kind of atmosphere works great for me. You might prefer working out by yourself at home or on a machine at the gym. There are many choices that fit your style.

Yoga is a fantastic exercise for men and women of all ages, and it is so good for many areas of the body. Yoga has been found to improve quality of life by reducing stress, anxiety, insomnia, depression, and back pain. It has also been found to lower heart rate and blood pressure and improve fitness, strength, flexibility, and balance. If you start yoga as a beginner, go to an introductory class. It will help you learn the poses and breathing techniques. I have what is known as a "monkey mind." (It just jumps all over the place), and I find it hard to rest and just breathe. I like hot flow yoga. It has all the typical yoga poses and breathing exercises, followed by a section of sequential poses done to music.

Warning: It's HOT yoga, meaning the room is heated high enough to loosen up the muscles, so you get a deep stretch. That also means you sweat, sweat, sweat, but you get used to it. Don't try this type first, and make sure you check with your doctor. Above all: please don't compare yourself to others in the class—some of those people can bend those bodies in unbelievable ways.

What sports or activities did you do as a younger person?

_____

_____

_____

What interests you now?

_____

_____

_____

What would be a really new activity you might try? Think outside the box here. (Aerial yoga, fencing, water polo, tap dancing, ball room dancing, or magic.)

_____

_____

_____

MOVE IT OR LOSE IT

The impact of movement—even leisurely movement can be beneficial. For starters, you'll burn more calories. This can lead to weight loss and increased energy. The muscle activity needed for standing and other movement seems to trigger important reactions related to the breakdown of fats and sugars within the body. When you sit, these responses do too—and your health risks increase. When you're standing or actively moving, you kick the processes back into action.

> "It is better to be tired from physical exertion than to be fatigued by the 'poisons' generated by nervousness while lying awake."
> – Joseph Pilates

In October 12, 2017, the Mayo Clinic News reported, "It's time to step away from the computer and read this: according to one study, people who spend more than four hours a day in front of a screen have a higher risk of early death in general and a higher risk of events related to heart disease, such as chest pain or heart attack."

It isn't the computer screen or the TV screen that is the concern. Any extended sitting—such as behind a desk at work or behind the wheel in your car—can be harmful. The solution? Sit less and move more overall. You might start by simply standing rather than sitting whenever you have the chance.

For example:

- Stand while talking on the phone or eating lunch.
- If you work at a desk for long periods of time, try a standing desk—or improvise with a high table or counter.
- Set your watch, iPhone, or timer every hour for a stretch or a few steps around the room.
- Stand while you are waiting for your turn. I bowl once a week, and when I do, I make it a habit not to sit down

between my turns; I stand and watch the bowlers or chat with my friends.

Most recommendations for any type of exercise are to get moderate exercise three to four times a week. This is a minimum! In the book *Younger Next Year*, the authors, Dr. Henry Lodge and Chris Crowley, recommend six days a week for the rest of your life. If you are a Fitbit advocate, get a minimum of 10,000 steps a day. An average person has a stride length of 2.1 to 2.5 feet. That means that it takes over 2,000 steps to walk one mile, and 10,000 steps would be almost five miles. A sedentary person may only average 1,000 to 3,000 steps a day. Whatever you do and however you do it: steps, swimming, or walking three days or seven, remember the most important thing is to "just do it."

Joe was an engineer in Uniontown, Ohio, just outside of Akron. He had been a high school athlete, participated in intramurals in college, and played recreational sports as an adult. Before they were married, his wife stood at her future mother-in-law's side to learn the recipes from her native Italy. Even with a life of homemade Italian food, Joe was never considered overweight in any way. His lifestyle, coupled with genetics, however, combined to change his life.

Laser Focused on Diet and Exercise:
How Major Heart Surgery Changed My Life

My retirement was not based on my dislike or dis-contentment with my job. I enjoyed my work and my coworkers. Rather, I looked forward to traveling and enjoying life even more fully in retirement. As the date approached, I became increasingly worried about how I might be able to adjust to a retirement lifestyle after nearly thirty-seven years of meaningful and rewarding employment. Urged on by my wife and family, I finally made the leap and began my retirement.

Immediately, changes occurred. We relocated to Ohio to be close to our grown children and growing number of grandchildren. We built a new home and we rekindled old friendships. My wife and I both felt healthy, and boredom was never a problem. My prior concerns about a smooth adjustment to retirement never became an issue.

My wife resumed her part-time nursing job in Ohio. We traveled and vacationed, and I became happily in-volved in golf and other recreational activities. Within a few short years, I was suddenly diagnosed with hy-pertension and a leaky heart valve. I was a candidate for major open-heart surgery to prevent a more tragic, and possibly life-ending, health event.

I was somewhat shocked that this might be hap-pening to me, as I had always been in generally good health. However, genetics plays the single biggest part in how anyone's health might evolve in time, and my father was no stranger to heart problems during his lifetime.

I thought not only about my own welfare but also about that of my wife and the prospect of how life might change for her, as well as my children, if I were no longer around. Having a month notice prior to my heart surgery, I was thinking of and dealing with my own mortality as I had never done before. All this led me to prayer and an increasingly closer relationship with my Christian faith. Although I had never lived a risky lifestyle, I knew that if all went well with my surgery, I had to make some significant lifestyle changes.

I traveled to a world-famous heart hospital with my wife and our two local children, and I felt as mentally prepared as I could be. During two prior visits to the hospital for testing and consultations, the medical team had prepared me well for the sequence of events that would occur. I no longer had doubts about what might happen to me during and after surgery, although I was as anxious as I had ever been in my life.

After a relatively short prep period, I remember arriving in surgery, and the surgical team did a great job of talking with me and putting my mind at ease as much as possible. After an eight-hour surgery, I remember only being awakened in the recovery room, still well medicated but thankful to God and to my surgical team that I was alive. I learned that I had survived an aortic valve replacement, a mitral valve repair, and five coronary artery bypasses.

I returned home and began to deal with my life going forward. After many weeks of rehab and heart health educational training, I knew that in the future, I had to become laser focused on exercise and a better diet to maximize my future health. Just as importantly, I became more focused on the love and happiness of my family, which by then had grown to include several more grandchildren.

Today, more than five years after my surgery, I am happy and in good health. I was never considered overweight, but I lost about twenty-five pounds, and I routinely exercise four to six days per week, involving both cardio and mild strength training. I dedicate more time and energy in cultivating an even closer relationship with my beloved family. At the age of seventy-two, I am extremely happy in retirement, and (as the saying goes), *"Life is good."*

YOU ARE WHAT YOU EAT

Let's move on to thinking about nutrition. This is probably my least favorite thing, rejecting some foods because they are empty calories or just not good for me. I'll be honest: I am addicted to Diet Coke. My family, medical people, and the internet all tell me, "Don't drink that stuff!" But I do.

I keep a large bottle of water with me in the car, and I drink water with meals, but I love my Diet Coke at about ten in the morning. Funny thing, I drink decaffeinated coffee and tea, but I need that little pick-me-up.

What about the rest of the food we put into our bodies? I sometimes wonder if eating more greens and drinking more water and adding turmeric to our meals is going to add to the good years of our life or prolong those months in the nursing home? I am choosing to act as if it will give me a better quality of life NOW. For me, some of it is vanity; I have a set "do not exceed" number for my weight, and I don't let myself get past it. I want to fit in the clothes I have and look the way I do and not gain weight that will affect my heart, blood pressure, diabetes, mind, and ultimately what I am physically able to do.

"You are what you eat, so don't be fast, easy, or fake."
– Anonymous

One easy suggestion I heard was "don't eat dead food." Obviously, that is not meat or fish. They do need to be dead, but eat greens, fruit, and vegetables rather than processed or created foods like pasta, cereal, fast food, salami, or TV dinners. You get the idea. It is hard to do that, especially for those of us who grew up with TV dinners being a time-saver that our mothers loved. Coca Cola was popularized in the 50s, and we have had Coke, potato chips, and McDonald's almost all our lives.

Another easy suggestion for proper nutrition or eating healthy is the "my plate strategy." Make an imaginary line down the middle of your plate. On one side, fill your plate with greens and/or fruit. The other half is split between a protein and a starch. This works if you are cooking or someone is cooking for you at dinner time. If you are alone, as I am, I do this most of the time but not always.

One rite of passage as we retire or approach retirement

ChooseMyPlate.gov

is the opportunity for a colonoscopy. Love that drink before-hand, don't you? When I had a colonoscopy, I went in as me and came out as my grandmother! I woke up to find a packet of Metamucil on my chest. Our Nebraska grandmother had a bottle of Metamucil on the ledge of the kitchen window over her sink. Pretty yellow cafe curtains fluttering in the breeze and a tablet of fiber every day. It was a shock to me to sud-denly realize I needed that Metamucil on my windowsill too!

With me, they had found some pockets of colitis, and I was told it was also called the twenty-first century disease. Processed white bread, instant mashed potatoes, and all the other food we eat, coupled with a somewhat stressful life-style, causes irritable bowel disease.

A trick I have perfected over the years (when my car au-tomatically goes into a fast food line; honestly, it wasn't me) is that I immediately throw away the top bun on a sandwich. Then I pick away at the bread on the bottom. I try not to get fries, but if I do, I have a few bites then throw the rest in the garbage bag in my car.

Instead of fast food burgers and fries, try sub sandwiches. With just a little care, you can add to the daily quota of vegetables with your meal. I like Subway for sandwiches and ask the staff to pull some of the bread off the loaf. They do so with a smile, and I load up on veggies—no cheese—and still try to skip some of the bread. See, I'm always playing a little game with it!

What many researchers are saying is that there are certain nutrients that we need to be sure we are getting: things we need more as we age. The Academy of Nutrition and Dietetics says older adults should pay special attention to their intake of calcium, vitamin D, vitamin B-12, potassium, and fiber.

Fortified milk and yogurt can boost calcium and vitamin D. Lean meat, fortified cereal, and some fish and seafood have vitamin B12. Fruits and vegetables also have potassium and fiber. This fiber thing is amazing: it makes you feel full, stops you from eating so much, and it's good for your colon. Oh my gosh, since when did we care about things being good for our colon?

A final comment on nutrition and longevity: *The Blue Zones*. These zones get their name from the blue pen used to draw circles that located the areas on a map. Since the 1990s, Dan Buettner has been traveling with teams of researchers to areas around the world where people live the longest. They observe how lifestyle and environment come into play. He has written three books and is working with Healthways to help cities and businesses in the USA make healthy changes. Information from his book is worth examining for what we can learn about a healthy retirement.

National Geographic had a television segment on Ikaria, Greece, a ninety-nine-square-mile island thirty miles off the coast of Turkey. After the first edition of Blue Zones was published in 2008, Buettner says Greek researchers contacted him about Ikaria.

"They gave us the tip that the island has ten times as many siblings over the age of ninety compared with any other place in Europe," says Buettner. "Then we got a grant from National Geographic to go there. The first expedition was to look at birth and death records. The second expedition was to tease out what's going on."

They confirmed the longevity numbers and found that those who live there also have less cancer, cardiovascular disease, depression, and dementia than other parts of Europe, and men outlive women. Those are certainly realities that merit our increased study and consideration.

In addition to eating a healthy Mediterranean diet (fruits, vegetables, whole grains, beans, nuts, healthy fats, and seafood), there are other key habits and values embraced by the Ikaria inhabitants. Buettner has seen those same habits in the other four blue zones: Sardinia, Italy; Nicoya Peninsula, Costa Rica; Loma Linda, California; and Okinawa, Japan.

OBSERVATIONS FROM THE BLUE ZONES

The folks that lived and prospered in these blue zones had the following things in common.

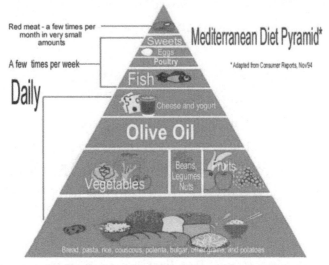

Mediterranean Diet Pyramid copyright @ 1994
Oldways Preservation and Exchange Trust.
Pyramid artwork and redesign copyright @1999 WHF

1. Movement was part of their day. It's not necessary to do marathons or pump iron unless that's your thing. Work around the house, walk, cycle, garden, and walk when you are on the phone.
2. They had a purpose. Have a reason for waking up in the morning. If you wake up, God still has a purpose for you. What is it?
3. They knew when to kick back. Find ways to shed stress, whether it's praying, napping, or going to happy hour.
4. They didn't eat a lot. Stop eating when you are 80% full. (Isn't this one hard?)

5. They didn't eat much meat. Beans are a cornerstone of most centenarians' diets.
6. They were moderate drinkers. Only the Seventh-day Adventists in California didn't have one to two glasses a day.
7. They had faith and religion. Denomination doesn't seem to matter, but attending faith-based services (four times a month) does.
8. They were surrounded by loved ones. Put families first, including committing to a partner and aging parents. It isn't always possible to live near parents as they age. If you aren't near them, try to call, Skype, or Facetime on a regular basis. The same goes for our children. As we become the ones who need to have contact with families, perhaps getting in the habit of regular phone visits now will keep those connections strong when we need them!
9. They were social. Build a social network that supports healthy behaviors. In many European communities (I'm thinking Spain, Italy, and Greece), I have seen men on the corners playing chess or checkers. The women congregate in the kitchen to share news. This keeps that social life strong and their minds active.

These lessons fall into the five areas first mentioned in the introduction: body, spirituality, mind, work, and relationships. You don't have to live in a blue zone to be healthy, just follow their tips.

Got it, rockstar? Do you know what areas of the body and

health you need to work on for your encore? Below is a questionnaire for you to take and see where your life is needing a little attention before this encore. Let's do it!

For maximum wellness, all the five major areas of life need to be addressed. It is okay if we are stronger in fitness than our social life, but we don't want to become isolated or deficient in any of these areas.

"An apple a day keeps the doctor away."
– Proverb

In the following exercise, the five primary areas of life are listed. Under each major heading are three statements. Mark one to five, with one being low or strongly disagree and five being high or strongly agree. After you complete the chart, compute your scores and use your average to mark the wheel. The first wheel is an example that shows how to place your scores.

1 Strongly disagree		**2** Disagree		**3** Not sure/ Neutral		**4** Agree		**5** Strongly agree	

Score	1	2	3	4	5

Social

I have a feeling of well-being and belonging.

I feel respected and treated fairly by my friends.

I have a plan for bettering relationships with people who are important to me.

Total Score

Average Score (Total divided by 3)

Spiritual

I act in ways that reflect my beliefs in right and wrong.

I have enough activities to make me feel worthwhile.

I have a plan for improving myself and contributing to the well-being of others.

Total Score

Average Score (Total divided by 3)

Physical

I eat well and exercise often.

I get outdoors and stay active.

I am satisfied with my physical health.

Total Score

Average Score (Total divided by 3)

Emotional

I am comfortable expressing my feelings.

I can manage my stress level.

My feelings about myself and my world are good.

Total Score

Average Score (Total divided by 3)

Mental

I take advantage of opportunities to learn new things.

I feel good when I learn new things about myself.

I know where to get help for my mental well-being if I need.

Total Score

Average Score (Total divided by 3)

Now take your scores and fill them in on this chart above.

The top wheel is an example for you.
Your own scores go on the bottom wheel.

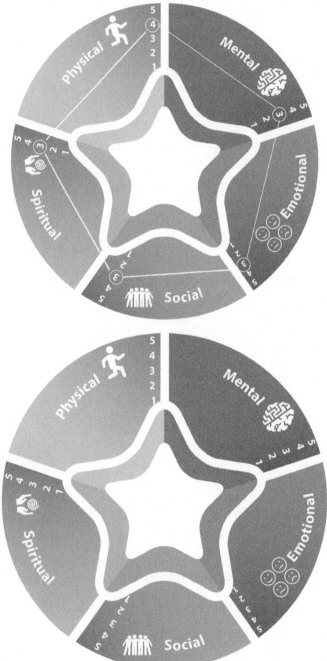

How did you do on the wheel? If you find there are areas that you think are low, try to make some small changes. Any change in one area will affect all the others, hopefully for the better. For example, when you are in better shape and feeling positive about your fitness and diet, your mental and emotional well-being increases. Make a reasonable, measurable goal and get started. A measurable goal would be: "I will have a gym membership by August," as opposed to, "I will get in better shape." Another measurable goal would be; "I will walk 45 minutes a day" rather than "I'll start walking." Your future health and finances, and the length and quality of your encore, all depend on this. Let's do it!

4
To Work or
Not to Work

When I asked a friend what retirement meant to her, she answered, "It's one big paid vacation!" After a few moments, she added, "but you need to have the money to live on so you can enjoy it."

There are numerous other books, articles, and people to help you with your portfolio and retirement investments. That is not the purpose of this book. I sincerely hope you have this vital step already covered, so you can have the kind of fun and lifestyle you want in your retirement. This is a VERY important part of your retirement. You must have your finances in order. In your encore years, you will most likely have twenty to twenty-five years to enjoy life. You need to have a financial plan in place in order to do so! Please see your financial advisor to make sure your money will last as long as you do.

Let's look into some tips on making the most of the money you do have. Income taxes rise and fall, and the amount allowed for deductions on health care is not fixed, so we need to be able to save or earn a little when we can. Always a good thing, right?

TO WORK OR NOT TO WORK, THAT IS THE QUESTION.

The answer? It's up to you! Since you have retired, I am guessing you are done with your full-time, lifelong career. Some people—teachers, engineers, consultants, and veterinarians, to name a few—retire, draw their pension, and then go back to the same job or the same field and work part-time. Others go to a completely different job. Others say, "Job? How do you spell that?" Whatever you choose, the variety and amount of possibilities for employing seniors is growing.

> "The quickest way to double your money is to fold it up and put it back in your pocket."
> - Will Rogers

Before taking on a new job, ask yourself these questions.

What is motivating you to find a retirement job? Money? Boredom? Both? You may use the spaces provided to write your answers.

- How much money do you need to earn? _____
  _____

- What do you want to have time to do?
  _____

- What kind of activities would you like to engage in at

work? _____

- What kind of work would you find fulfilling?
  _____

- How much time do you want to spend on the job?
  _____

- Will you work part-time or full-time? _____

- How much responsibility do you want? _____
  _____

- How much flexibility do you want? _____
  _____

- Would you consider working for yourself? _____
  _____

- What kind of retraining are you willing to engage in?
  _____

I once saw a listing for a part-time park ranger job that was just Saturdays and Sundays. That sounded good to me, especially since it was summer. At the interview, I discovered it wasn't seasonal; it was all year. I live in Denver and to reach the location, I'd have to drive up to the top of a nearby mountain. That nixed it for me right away. Besides, I value my independence and enjoy traveling. A job in which someone is relying on me to meet their schedule every day is not a good fit. You need to decide if a schedule or flexibility works best for you.

My perfect job is dog and house sitting. I have made a modest amount of money in the last year by staying in a nice house with my own dog and theirs. It is flexible, and I do it on my schedule. If I have plans that take me out of town, I don't accept the job—a great gig for my encore income.

The average charge is forty dollars a day, which is quite reasonable, and you could charge that or more in many neighborhoods. If you don't want the overnight scene, you could offer to just feed and walk the dog. Rover.com is a website that acts as a liaison between people offering pet services and those who are looking for help.

Because the number of baby boomers is staggering, both businesses and industry are being more accommodating to the retirement plans of some employees. Phased retirement allows you to stay at your current job while working less hours. This is good for passing on the experience of senior workers to the younger ones— a win-win for everyone. If your company doesn't offer that yet, you could promote yourself as a consultant. Many retired educators do that as well.

MaryEllen, seventy, was a nurse and a widow. Upon retirement, she experienced a period of loss and a lack of identity. After a respite of grace and adjustment, she realized she needed reinvention and a part-time job. Fortunately for MaryEllen, local businesses were looking for older, experienced workers.

I was an RN for forty-nine years (graduated in 1969 and always worked, even if it was part-time.) During my career, I was able to reinvent myself many times. I did all types of rotations: Pediatrics, ER, Burn Unit, Medical Surgery, Hospice, home care, supervisor, and the Clinical Review Team. Thus, I was never bored.

I was living and working in Florida when my husband died suddenly. Two of my daughters lived in Denver, and my third daughter lived in California. They urged me to move to be closer to them and my grandchildren. I retired and made the move to Denver. With the retirement, I no longer had the initials "RN" as part of my identity. I felt lost and empty, and a feeling of grief overcame me. Now what would I do with the rest of my life? I was retired for a year, and in spite of church activities, volunteer opportunities, spending time with my grandchildren, reading, and watching TV, it just was not enough. I was spending too much time alone. It was time to reinvent myself again. I was over death and dying and needed a new focus.

At that point, I decided to get a job. I wanted to do something to get me out of the house and with people on a regular basis. I love to shop, so I chose to get a part-time job in retail. It is a reason to get up, dress up, and go have fun. This job is a delight. The store looks and smells so good. Beats the inside of a hospital. Loved my nursing career, but it was just too emotionally and physically draining. I found out that I could get a part-time job in about three minutes, hired on the spot—my age bracket was not an issue and my customers can relate to me. We have life experiences we can offer to employers, and I am so happy with my choice to be an active part of life!

START YOUR OWN BUSINESS

From running a bed and breakfast to launching a new product, retirees are starting their own businesses in droves. Retirees are involved in online work, whether writing blogs or selling products; the internet is hot. If the internet is not your thing, there are a wide variety of options for you when looking to develop a small business. For example:

- A teacher might tutor, write curriculum or workbooks, consult, or teach a few online courses, as online education is becoming more and more popular.
- A retired police or law enforcement person could offer safety or self-defense classes or a class in fraud prevention.
- A person who likes meeting people might try hotel reception or campground hosting.
- Frontier Airlines has a "scout" position in which the employee works part-time doing PR work in the airport. (You get employee flight benefits with that too.)
- Do you fish or play golf? You might offer lessons in your neighborhood or volunteer with Boy Scouts or Girl Scouts.
- Are you a shopper? A secret shopper position is another option. If you like shopping, this could be a perfect job for you.

If you are thinking of starting your own business, maybe out of your home, one source for advertising is the website Nextdoor. (www.nextdoor.com)

This is an informational website for your particular neighborhood. On this website, you can advertise furniture or services you have for sale, offer yourself as a pet sitter or tutor, or just express concern over happenings in your neighborhood. It's actually a bit like the bush telephone in Africa; all the news is on it. Last week, in my neighborhood Nextdoor site, there was a post about a dead skunk, a speeding truck, and a neighbor in search of someone to build a deck. Anything you want to sell, buy, or inform others about: Nextdoor is the place!

"H and R Block hires tax preparers in the US. They also offer a free course for applicants to get the training needed."

TRAVEL JOBS

For many people, retirement and traveling are synonymous. If this is you, perhaps you can earn a little income while seeing the world. There are many ads for travel writers. If you like traveling and writing, or you are a good photographer, this is worth considering. Another wonderful opportunity is becoming a trip organizer, where you would help as a guide or coordinator on a trip. Do some research by calling some travel companies. The perk is your spot on the trip is free or offered at a reduced rate. Some travel companies offering these positions are:

- EF GoAhead Tours (www.goaheadtours.com)
  If you get six people, your spot is free.
- Cruise Only (www.cruisesonly.com/Group-Cruises)
  If you bring eight people, you go free.
- Overseas Adventure Travel (www.oattravelcom)
  You go free after the eighth person or receive $100 for the first three people you refer, and you get incrementally higher rewards up to the eighth person.

- Want to be a flight attendant? It's not out of the realm of possibility. Southwest Airlines, among others, occasionally opens for external applicants, and they have been hiring job seekers who are fifty-plus.
- Can you dance? If you are a man, cruise ships hire people to dance with all the single ladies! In fact, cruise ships have many positions other than cabin attendants and bartenders.
- Are you an expert in history, geography, art, or other culturally related areas?

Cruise lines hire people who lecture on a topic of interest based on the location the cruise is going to visit. In return for providing lectures, their berth is free. A recent ad for Carnival Cruise Line read:

"This is a great opportunity for recently retired individuals, such as teachers and university professors. Successful candidates will be knowledgeable about the geography, ecology, history, etc. of the cruise itinerary and ports of call. Guest speakers will be friendly with an outgoing personality and have experience in adult education and leading group tours."

Some internet sites that can help you find these possibilities (and more) are:

- **Teach Abroad** (www.goabroad.com)
  Might you be qualified to teach English abroad? Among the jobs that pay well, teaching English is one that also gives you the opportunity to see other parts of the world.
- **Cool Works** (www.coolworks.com)
  Job listings for working in great places like national

parks, dude ranches, great lakes, and more. There are job postings in every state—pretty cool way to see the great beauty in our country.

- **Summer Jobs** (www.summerjobs.com)
  Find fun seasonal work.

- **Carnival Cruise Line** (www.carnival.com)
  Set sail! The world at sea is yours.

- **Workamper** (www.workamper.com)
  Have you ever considered being a campground host? How about doing construction work at a campsite? An activity director or musician or attendant at the petting zoo? The only thing those who are called "workampers" seem to have in common is they travel in RV's, not that they work in camps. The opportunities are many and varied; take a look!

- **Transitions Abroad** (www.transistionsabroad.com)
  Employment or a place to live or travel abroad is what they offer. Jobs include tour guide, student advisor, staff assistant, writer, and more. At this writing, Transitions Abroad had 171 jobs listed.

> "Life begins at the end of your comfort zone."
> - Neale Donald Walsch

DON'T BREAK THE BANK WHEN YOU TRAVEL.

Katie Brockman, writing for The Motley Fool, says that 40% of retirees surveyed indicate that travel is more expensive than they planned. Add to that, newly retired people take approximately four trips a year and spend over $11,000 on travel.

Want to figure out how to travel and rock it at the same time? Discounts are available in many different forms. AARP members get discounts from hotel chains, Expedia, Windstar Cruises, and other companies. Do you have a Costco membership? Discount travel is available through them. Don't forget AAA; that card also is well known for getting discounts. Some airlines, like United and Southwest, also offer discounts for seniors.

Use the in-between times, or "shoulder season," for less expensive rates on flights and rooms. For example, travel during times other folks are staying home. Dude ranches in Colorado offer cheaper rates in April and early May before the season starts and in September and October before winter sets in. Take trips overseas in May or September when you can, and don't go in August as that's when Europeans vacation, especially to France. Right after New Year's is also a good time for travel, as everyone has overspent on Christmas and the holidays.

Open an account, like a health savings account (HSA), just for your travel. Pull your travel money from there and be strict about it. Even if you use your charge card to get more mileage points or cash back rewards, know what your bills will be and then transfer just that amount into your charge card account.

WHAT ROLE DOES YOUR HOUSE PLAY?

You had your dream house when you were thirty with three kids, and you frequently hosted the neighborhood Cub Scout pack or the cheer team. Now, it's just the two of you. What has your house become in your retired life?

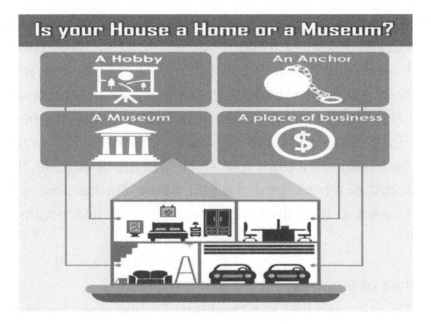

Is your House a Home or a Museum?

A Hobby · An Anchor · A Museum · A place of business

A Hobby

There is enough money in your retirement account, and you have already paid off the house. You enjoy renovation, and you are big on DIY. You want to choose new paint colors, and your husband wants to lay new flooring before his back gets worse. You both love to garden. While he likes vegetables, your love is flowers. Your home is a place to occupy your time in retirement.

A Museum

The children are gone and have moved to other parts of the country. Their bedrooms look the way they did when the kids were in high school. In your garage are sleds they used on snowy hills and old bicycles that have survived the years. The thought of moving away from the memorabilia and locale is unbearable.

An Anchor

Four bedrooms, a living room, family room, three baths, and a two-car garage are keeping you from having your dreams. You think of living in Panama or Italy, but the house needs so much repair work done, it is cutting into your budget for a meaningful and enjoyable retirement. You would like to travel in an RV, but you can't afford to buy one with the high cost of repairs needed on the house. Furthermore, you don't want to have the house unattended for five months a year.

A Place of Business

Do you run a bed and breakfast? Do you make things to sell or teach classes from your home? Do you work online? Perhaps you are a hair stylist, work remotely for offices, do tax preparation, or perform medical transcription.

Take a look at your current situation with your house and consider how these questions affect your life in your current living situation.

- Is it enjoyable? Can you afford it? Or is it keeping you from experiencing new things in your retirement? If you sell it and move, consider these points:
- Need friends? An active adult or retirement community might be of interest.
- Need family? Move nearer to the kids.
- Need adventure? It's time to travel, camp, or get that RV.
- Single? Don't become isolated. You can find friends, travel opportunities, or learn new hobbies at senior

centers, churches, or libraries: all good ways to connect with people.

BEING AN EXPAT

For some people, living out of the US is part of the thrill of retirement and part of the adventure they want to have. Living abroad can be really inexpensive and a great way to stretch the dollar, giving you a chance to really rock your retirement.

"So, when is this 'old enough to know better' supposed to kick in?"
– Anonymous

International Living (www.internationalliving.com) lists ten places each year that are economical, safe, and fun for Americans to live. Some of those are:

MALTA:	$2,700 per month per couple
NICARAGUA:	$1,500 per month per couple
MALAYSIA:	$2,000 per month per couple
MEXICO:	$2,500 per month per couple

San Miguel Allende has a large community of Americans and is just one of several locations in Mexico. Todos Santos outside of Cabo San Lucas is another.

In many of these places, the above numbers represent rent, food, entertainment, and medical care. For some people, inexpensive health care that can be found abroad is a big draw. For example, in Malaysia, a man reported having a torn anterior cruciate ligament repaired—hospital, anesthesia, drugs, and all—for about $2,000. In the US, $18,000 is more likely what one would pay.

(www.internationalliving.com/knee-surgery)

Many of these countries have special discounts for seniors

in addition to the low cost of living. Because these locations have a large expatriate community, you are not alone and have many resources from which to draw. WARNING! If you are a US citizen living abroad, you still have to pay US taxes on income, as well as local taxes. However, if you want your encore to really rock and have a short-term adventure, this may be a good opportunity!

How does a winter home in Todos Santos, Mexico and a summer home in Bear Mountain, California sound to you? Tom and Deb tried this lifestyle before they retired in an effort to test the waters in ex-pat living. Here is their story.

Both were working as educational researchers and speakers (nationally and internationally). When Tom retired at sixty-two, Deb was not yet ready. After seeing Tom in the hot tub early in the morning as she bustled off to work, it didn't take long before she said, "Hey, wait! I want to play too!" They found a thriving community outside of Cabo San Lucas with the ocean, beaches, a modest farm community, and sand dunes for off-road biking. In addition, Colorado State University offers continuing education in nearby Tres Santos. There are artists, yoga classes, restaurants, an English book store, African drumming, and tai chi. With seasonal film and music festivals, what more could you want? The locals are friendly, and there are opportunities for volunteering by teaching English to schoolkids or playing soccer at a nearby orphanage.

When it starts to get hot, Tom and Deb load up the

car and return to California and the mountains. They have a small cabin near Bear Valley that used to be their ski cabin. With a small lake next to their cabin, they realized how much they like it there in the summers. They hike, kayak, read, and relax. Their extended family comes up in August for a yearly reunion. Although the cabin is small, tents pop up outside along the lake, and everyone enjoys the pines and the California mountain lifestyle. Their ex-pat life has the best of both worlds!

SCHOOL'S OUT FOREVER—OR NOT

The Department of Education states that more than half a million men and women over fifty are part or full-time students in undergraduate and graduate programs in the US. Many more seniors take training programs and vocational education, as well as courses merely for their own interest.

When making a career switch around retirement, it is important to consider how much time and money the education will cost and whether or not the outlay is commensurate with the financial or other benefits you will receive.

Charlie works summers at concert venues in Denver. As he is tall and silver- haired, I—of course—found my way over to interview him. He was working as security for a country western group in Colorado. A great job, by the way, if you like music, crowds, and people. I approached him to ask if he was retired, and he said "No." I looked at him quizzically, as he looked old enough to be retired, and he said, "I'm in med school."

Okay. My expression was one of amazement, I'm sure. When I asked about the cost and time he was putting in at this stage of his life, his answer floored me. "I want to serve the poorest of the poor." He was going to school in the Caribbean and was prepared to give the next seven years to reach his goal. He had, in fact, retired from a previous job and was recently widowed. Life insurance and a paid-off house, which he sold, financed his medical school education. When school is not in session, Charlie comes to Denver and lives with his son. (Talk about a role reversal.) Charlie could have traveled or played golf, but he had a passion for helping people and was smart enough to pass the MCATs. He chose not to go home and sit down but created a challenging path for his early retirement years. As of this writing, Charlie has one more year of med school before residency and interning. For his encore years, Charlie is starting a new career and helping people at the same time. What a way to rock your retirement!

You may be facing retirement from one job, but many people take this opportunity to truly make a difference in their encore career. That difference can be in furthering your education in a new field or helping the poor in impoverished areas with skills you acquired at your lifelong job. Charlie's encore has him spending quite a bit of time, effort, and finances. It is not for everyone, but his story shows it can be done with desire and persistence. Retirement from one job can certainly lead you to another—if you choose.

How Big is Your Piggy Bank?

"You get a discount, you get a discount, and you get a discount!" (Read this in an Oprah Winfrey voice.) Whoever said getting older was a bad thing obviously didn't know about these fantastic senior discounts! AARP has hundreds of ways to save money, so be sure to check out their website frequently.

> "Will you look back on life and say, 'I wish I had' or 'I'm glad I did'?"
> - Zig Zigler

Other sources are The Penny Hoarder, Retailmenot, and Senior Citizen Discount List. Another place which lists retailers offering discounts (restaurants, grocery stores, car companies and more) is Brad's Deals. To get an idea of the vast number and types of discounted merchandise and opportunities, all which range from 5-10%, here is a sampling of places that offer discounts.

Restaurant Discounts
- Applebee's
- Bonefish Grill
- Boston Market
- Bubba Gump Shrimp Company
- Chili's
- Denny's
- Dunkin' Donuts
- Fazolli's
- Friendly's Restaurant
- Golden Corral
- IHOP
- McCormick and Schmick's

- The Oceanaire Seafood Room
- Outback Steakhouse
- Old Country Buffet
- The Old Spaghetti Factory
- Shoney's of Knoxville
- Sizzler
- Subway
- Sweet Tomatoes

All fast food places offer some type of discount, even if it's "senior coffee" at half the price.

Retail and Clothing Discounts
- Banana Republic
- Bealls
- Belk
- Bon-Ton Department Stores
- Kohl's
- LensCrafters: AARP members get 30% off a complete pair of eye glasses and 40% off a complete pair of transition lenses.
- Tanger Outlets: Free coupon book for AARP
- Stein Mart: Every first Monday of the month, when signed up on their website as a member, they email their customers (55+) with coupons valid for that Monday only. Discounts vary month-to-month.
- Dress Barn

Travel Discounts
- Publix: 5% discount on Wednesdays (60+) at select

locations.
- American Airlines: various discounts for 65+ (call before booking for discount).
- Amtrak: 15% off (62+).
- Auto Europe: 5% senior discount.
- British Airways: AARP members can save anywhere from $65-$200 on flights.
- Carnival Cruise: Exclusive savings vary for senior citizens (55+).
- Greyhound: 5% off (62+).
- Hilton Hotels and Resorts: AARP members receive up to 10% off the best available rate.
- InterContinental Hotels Group: Discounts vary for senior citizens (62+).
- Marriott Hotels: 15% off (62+).
- Motel 6: 10% off (60+).
- Myrtle Beach Resort: 10% off (55+).
- Royal Caribbean: Reduced senior prices on select sailings
- (55+).
- Airlines : Various discounts for ages 65+ (call before booking for discount).

Many hotel chains offer discounts through AARP or simply saying you are a senior. In my research, I have found that being with AARP or AAA has more discounts than simply saying "I'm a senior," although that does work too.

- Clarion
- Comfort Inn
- Comfort Suites

- Econo Lodge
- Hampton Inn
- Hilton Hotels
- Holiday Inn
- Hyatt Hotels
- Mainstay Suites
- Marriott Hotels
- Motel 6
- Quality Inn
- Red Roof Inn

Entertainment Discounts

- MoviePass: For a yearly joining fee of $120, you can go to the movies every day of the year. It operates like club membership for all regular movies with an additional fee of $10 a month.
- Cinemark, Regal and AMC offer their own discount membership plans for movie fans.
- Matinees and special discount days
- SeaWorld Parks: Specials on annual passes (65+).
- US National Parks: 50% off services, including camping (62+).

Miscellaneous Discounts

- AT&T: AARP members save 10% on qualified plans.
- Great Clips: Senior discounts vary by location.

Since many senior discounts are not advertised to the public, my advice to anyone over fifty-five is ALWAYS ask a sales associate if that store provides a senior discount. Some senior discounts vary by region, some by day of the week. Really, it seems to me that by merely ASKING almost everywhere, you can save a little cash. If we do this consistently, it will add up!

Speaking of "adding up," Marjie and Bernie, both seventy-two, from Gilbert, Arizona, relate how they managed their money from the very early days of their careers until retirement. Their story shows how, as Marjie stated, "living frugally" throughout their life enabled them to spend their retirement years without working a second job or stressing about how they were going to pay for it.

In our twenties, my husband and I were members of the California State Teachers' Retirement System, then members of the Arizona State Retirement System. We viewed these two automatic memberships in terms of our short-term desire to minimize deductions allowing take-home salary to be maximized. Retirement was a long way off.

In our thirties, when I worked for a law firm and my husband was still teaching at the community college, we continued to see retirement in the distant future. I contributed the allowable amount to the retirement plan, so I could receive the maximum match. He contributed an affordable amount to the Retirement System and to private investments.

In our forties, our investments grew, and we paid

little attention to our accounts since, still, retirement was a long way off. We worked. We raised two children. We wondered if we were saving too much.

Then we reached our fifties. We started dreaming of retirement: How soon? How to afford it? What could we do with our time? Could we really leave our jobs to someone else who might not perform them as well as we had? And then, we focused on reality: We planned to pay for our two children's college educations. We had to keep working, spending sparingly, paying tuition, and saving. We found a way to ease into retirement by working part-time. We enjoyed this arrangement for a few years, and then cut the cord to grasp free time while we were young and healthy enough to enjoy it.

Now in our very early seventies, we travel each summer in our Airstream trailer. We escape the hothouse of Arizona, explore the wonders of North America, hike in state and national parks, photograph nature, and visit friends and relatives. When we arrive home in the fall, we reacquaint ourselves with our neighbors and friends, volunteer in the community, enjoy making improvements in our house and yard, read books, travel to see our children, talk about how retirement keeps us busy, and toy with the idea of traveling in Europe. We think our savings, investments, and social security will last for a long time if we keep spending sparingly and if fortune continues to shine on us.

ONE CAR FOR TWO PEOPLE?

A friend in Denver told me that she and her husband each sold their cars and bought a truck to pull their Airstream. I was aghast! "You sold your car? You have to share a car and a schedule?" She told me it actually causes them to have an intentional conversation each evening, as they go over who needs to be where and when. She said the money it saves in insurance, repairs, and gas is pretty noticeable.

Cut the Cable

Using cable TV can cost $100–150 or more a month. There are many ways to enjoy your TV shows at a fraction of the cost. From HBO and Netflix to Sling TV or an indoor antenna, your choices just depend on how you watch TV. If it's mostly network shows that you enjoy, an indoor antenna can cost you around ten dollars.

If you crave sports or the cooking channel, Sling.com seems like a great way to get the TV you want at an à la carte format. Costing between twenty to forty dollars, you get from twenty-five to forty channels of your choosing. Using Time.com will help you navigate the maze of options for lower cost TV.

"If you don't want to work [in retirement], you have to work to earn enough money so that you won't have to work."
– Ogden Nash

Happy Hour

Not just for alcohol, happy hour is a great time for small bites for dinner. Instead of twenty-five dollars each for your meal, you can get it at half that price. Some restaurants have a Twilight Menu for seniors at the five to six o'clock hour, or you can order a regular meal and share it! Don't forget to check out Groupon (wwww.groupon.com), as they often have restaurants offering discounted deals.

Insurance

Your Medicare supplement may be siphoning off more than you need. Check this each year. You might find that there is another plan with a cheaper monthly premium or lower deductibles. Remember, kicking your bad habits like smoking, not exercising, and eating junk food can save you money on medical care too!

Car Insurance

Those companies are always looking for new enrollees, and the bids are competitive. To make things super easy, you can "talk" to a bot on Facebook Messenger! In February, 2017 Digital Trends reported, "Our Facebook Messenger virtual agent experience is faster than any website or mobile app, and easier to use than any online form," said Snejina Zacharia, Insurify's founder and CEO." Users can upload pictures of their license plate, answer a few questions, and have multiple quotes in minutes. Sure sounds better than filling out a postcard and getting multiple calls and emails from random agents for months.

HOW MUCH MONEY DO YOU NEED?

The type of job you choose, trips you take, or fun you have after retirement will likely be at least somewhat determined by your financial situation. Do you know what your financial needs are? Today? Twenty years from now? The NewRetirement Calculator is a retirement tool that is easy to use but highly detailed as a resource. It lets you create your own retirement plan and keep it updated. You can enter different income and expense levels for various time periods.

"I have enough money to last me the rest of my life, unless I buy something."
– Jackie Maso

This tool was recently named the best retirement calculator by the American Association of Individual Investors and *Forbes Magazine*. You can find this retirement tool and others at the New Retirement website. (www.newretirement.com)

Jobs

Employers are actively seeking seniors as purchasers for their products and as employees to sell them. You might be surprised by the range of companies with jobs for seniors. Everyone from McDonalds to CVS Pharmacies and New York Life Insurance wants to employ older Americans (finally). *AARP Magazine* (October, 2017) stated that businesses prefer the experience, mature skills, and temperament of older workers.

AARP has developed a program called the AARP's Best Employers Program. For this program, AARP partnered with employers who want the experience and leadership of older Americans. (www.AARP.org/work)

Visit the following links for more information about companies seeking seniors.

- RetiredBrains.com: This site offers seniors and retirees

the opportunity to search for a job and/or post their resume at no charge. Employers looking to hire older workers for full-time, part-time, and temporary jobs or for project assignments list their openings. There is also a searchable database for those with the experience and skills to match their openings.

- Careers at 50+ from Monster.com
- Senior Job Bank
- Seniors for Hire

Volunteering

There are so many worthy causes in the world and not nearly enough people to serve them: hospitals, schools, libraries, churches, parks, zoos, international relief organizations, and more. Many seniors are already participating in these types of endeavors. For example, the Peace Corps reports that 7%—about 450—of their volunteers are over fifty years of age.

If interesting work and vitality are more important to you than income, volunteering may be the right and most rewarding option for keeping you busy and offering meaning to your encore years. The following organizations offer special programs for seniors. You can also google "Volunteering in _____." (Insert the name of your city in the blank.)

- Senior Corps
- Encore
- Senior Corps Foster Grandparent Program
- Senior Corps Retired and Senior Volunteer Program
- Volunteer Match

- Volunteers of America
- Experience Corps
- Volunteers in Parks Program, National Park Service
- The Peace Corps

Volunteering at venues as an usher allows you to see plays and concerts free. If you are a fan of live music and drama, this is a great way to enjoy it.

There are many agencies looking for help and you will find many sites listing times and qualifications that best match the volunteer positions you find interesting.

A part-time job, school, or volunteering can all contribute to making your encore years more enjoyable. Whatever you choose to do, you have the freedom to change if it doesn't feel right. Give it a try. This life is yours to live!

"I joined the Peace Corps when I was fifty-six years old, and it was like having a second life. As I got older, I began to think less about 'me' and more about 'we.' I loved working for the Peace Corps; I felt like I did something for the world, for the planet."
- Diana Gomez, Returned Peace Corps Volunteer, Armenia

"My wife and I served from 2005 to 2007 in Botswana after retirement at age fifty-five! It was one of the interesting and rewarding experiences of our lives! I encourage all older folks to consider the Peace Corps, and enjoy working with wonderfully idealistic young Americans who share common visions."
- David Hartley

- **Transitions Abroad** (www.transistionsabroad.com)
  This site lists jobs that enable you to live, work, and travel abroad. Some such positions are tour guide,

student advisor, staff assistant, writer, and many more. Transitions Abroad had 171 jobs listed last year.

If traveling is a goal, and you have always planned on retiring and seeing the world (and you are too old for the Navy), now is a good time to make some plans. You may have a list of the places you wanted to see and experience or you may not. Take a look at the maps below and mark them up. Put in your "definitely want to go there places" and use another color for "maybe we can make it here too!" Then, you and your partner, if he or she is traveling with you, may need to answer some questions in order to make this dream a reality.

How will you get there?
- Trip
- Vacay
- Motor home

Who will go with you?
- Partner
- Friend
- Alone

When will you go?
It's a big world; explore it and enjoy it!

5

Five Friends
and a Hobby

When my friend Bob Felux told his doctor that he planned on retiring soon, the doctor replied, "Make sure you have five friends and a hobby so you don't drive your wife crazy."

Good advice, whether you are married or not. It is so important to have connections: relationships that sustain us, entertain us, and keep us grounded.

Consider the consequences of a silent disease that is creeping across the country: Its negative health effects are equal to smoking fifteen cigarettes a day, being an alcoholic, or being sedentary. It is twice as bad for retirees as obesity, but almost no one talks about this silent killer in retirement.

What is it? Loneliness. One in five people reports being lonely and the numbers increase as you age. Make keeping friendships or making new ones a priority as if your health depended on it—because it does. According to Dr. Andrea Bonoir in Friendship 2.0, real friends can help boost your immune system and lower your blood pressure. Friendships also reduce the risk of depression and anxiety that can come with the transitioning from a career to retirement. If you are married or have a committed partner, that alleviates some of the threat of loneliness. All of us, however, married or single, need to have good friends whom we can call on for laughter or commiseration, as the case may be.

This same smart doctor also said, "Have several things that YOU do, not just with your wife. You'll have together time, so it's important to have your own interests too." In a marriage, things can change or get sticky when retirement comes around.

"Less than 20% of couples retire at the same time."
- Center for Retirement Research, 2013

When one partner is still working, he or she tends to be a little jealous of the freedom of the one who is seen as being at home "playing." It usually doesn't take long for the other partner to decide it's time for him to retire too. This brings another set of complications.

TURF WAR

If you've been home a year or so before your spouse, you are used to the house being empty and having the run of the place. Suddenly, someone else is there twenty-four hours a day. It definitely helps to sit down and talk about each of your expectations. Here are a few areas you should talk about:

- Is the meal preparation, cleaning, and yard work still done by the person who did it before?
- Should one of you have the garage for hobbies and a man cave and the other get the spare room for their separate space?
- How much together and alone time are you planning on having?
- Will your schedules be the same? That is, will you go to bed and get up at the same time? One of my friend's husband just retired, and he wakes up but doesn't get up and out of bed for another hour or so. It drives her slightly crazy!

FOR BETTER OR WORSE

A Cornell study in 2001 said that men and women reported the highest marital conflict and lowest marital satisfaction immediately after they stopped working. The good news is that after two years or so they were very happy. What does that mean for you?

- Talk about it, even if one of you finds talking about those things difficult; you need to communicate.
- Be patient with yourself and each other as you navigate these new days.
- Keep your outside connections, so you can have other outlets.
- Plan on together time like date nights and vacations.
- Keep your need for alone time in the picture too.

Author and former financial planner Frank Maselli tells of a man who retired and went home to spend his days with his wife. It didn't take long for him to become a major intrusion into his wife's world. He began telling her everything she did wrong, even the garden she had tended for twenty-five years. She had to kick him out of the house and told him to get involved with a charity group and start going to the gym.

MEN AND WOMEN ARE DIFFERENT

Geoffrey Grief, PhD, from University of Michigan has found that men and women are different in the way they make friends and what they do with their friends. Men tend to make friends with whom they are "shoulder to shoulder," whether it's on a football team, the military, or at work. They might be at a bar watching a game, shoulder to shoulder looking at the screen, and catching up during commercials. Women, on the other hand, orchestrate and nurture their meetings with each other. Those friendships require maintenance with repeated contact and quality time, and women seem to love putting the effort into that.

If your retirement has you losing that core group of friends you had, or if you move to a new location, it is harder to make friends now than it was in your twenties. This is a time when you are going to have to be more assertive and make the first move. Do you go to the gym and smile or talk to the person standing next to you? Ask them to go for coffee with you a time or two? Do you sit at the same place at church each week? Do the same thing there, ask someone for coffee after the service. Social media and hitting "LOL" or "like" after reading an entry from a "friend" (whom you may have never met or never see in real life) cannot replace a face-to-face (or even voice-to-voice) conversation with someone. Reach out to your best friends from high school or college days. Those big reunions are coming up, and you will enjoy spending time with them more if you have kept your connections up-to-date. If you haven't, now is a good time to reestablish them.

Make sure you treasure them. If you are active and mobile, it is preferable to see your friends, not just message them via Facebook. However, some of us begin to have mobility problems and can't get out of the house for bridge at the senior center. If that is happening to you, you can call Dial-A-Ride or another agency that provides transportation to seniors for everyday errands. Also, with a housebound individual, having internet and instant messenger friends helps alleviate the feeling of loneliness. If you can get out and see your friends, please keep doing so. If you are unable to, by all means, maintain your internet connections.

> "It takes a lifetime to grow an old friend."
> – John Leonard

Keep up a sense of community. It may no longer be your community at work and not even at church or the neighborhood, especially if you move. Community can be any group you want. Do you go to Starbucks each day for coffee and internet? Strike up a conversation there. Do you volunteer at the same place? You already have something in common, so go out for a beer or wine sometime. What about the people you see at the gym? You can go out and commiserate about the hard work the instructor is making you do. Your health, both physical and mental, will be better for it.

In 2013, Merrill Lynch and Age Wave (MLAW) conducted a study asking pre-retirees what they would "miss most about work when they retire." What do you think they said? The answer? A steady income.

However, when the same question was asked of those who are already retired, the results were different. The variables "social connections," "having purpose," and "mental stimulation" in the MLAW survey account for 65% of the most regrettable losses retirees face in their post-work lives. That tells us there's a glaring contrast between what we think is important in retirement while we're still working and what's actually important once we reach that stage.

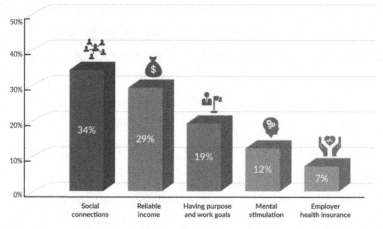

BASE : RETIREES

HOBBY LOBBY?

What about that hobby that the family doctor mentioned to Bob Felux? It can be something you do alone in the garage; in your chair; or golfing, bowling, or hiking—something that gets you out, away, and with other people. Some hobbies that can be done alone are knitting, quilt making, mosaics, fly tying, or making a ship in a bottle. You can try your hand at a musical instrument or join a choral group.

The majority of retirees say their enjoyment depends more on whom they do an activity with than on what they're doing. If the choice is between golfing alone or cleaning up trash with your kids and grandkids, most retirees will gladly throw on a pair of gloves and collect litter.

That's one aspect of what MLAW defines as "the new social security": "the value that social relationships add to mental, and even physical, health."

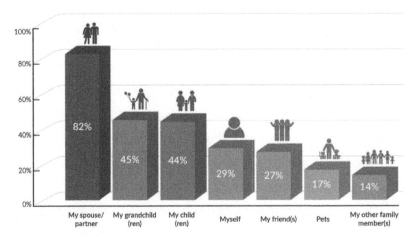

BASE : AGE 50+ RETIREES ; WITH RELATIVE ; BASES VARY

Single retirees have a slightly different pattern for people with whom they prefer to spend time. It is no surprise that friends replace "spouse" in the number one spot. Interestingly "myself" comes in at number two for singles but in married people "myself" comes in at number four. Single people have learned to be content while alone and often report that they do not possess a feeling of loneliness.

Another friend who makes lunches for the homeless every Monday said, "For better or worse but not for lunch." Meaning, hubby dear: you plan your day, and I'll plan mine, but lunch is not part of it. A mentor of mine often said to her family, "Are your hands painted on?" You want lunch, make it; don't sit at home while I'm at the gym and wait for me to get home. Another friend said, "The first day of my husband's retirement, I made sure I had a reason to leave the house. When I got home, we passed each other in the garage; he was on his way out to a movie that he knew I wouldn't want to see." Good move, Joe.

THE FOUNTAIN OF YOUTH

Admit it or not, we all want to feel young and vibrant. If it's a physical youth you want to maintain, hair dye and plastic surgery are available. If that's okay with you, go for it. Two generations ago, orthodontics was not heard of much. If your kid had bad teeth, well, they had bad teeth for life. In the late 50s orthodontics was becoming more accepted and now, especially in our western culture, nice, straight teeth are as expected and accepted as much as a measles vaccine. I think in the generations to come, plastic surgery and other means to keep the face fresh and young looking will be more widely done. After all, if a knee wears out, a new metal one is put in. If your gallbladder is bad, it gets removed. Wrinkles on the face? If you don't like them, get rid of them.

On an emotional level of keeping young and vibrant, doctors and members of the Silver Sneakers community state there are several ways to keep that feeling.

1. Hang out with people of mixed ages

Make sure you socialize with older and younger people. With younger folks, you will keep seeing the world through their eyes; be sure NOT to say, "Well, in MY day." Instead, listen and learn. Maybe the time will come to share your opinions. If you only hang out with the other retirees, that is the only way you see the world. Of course, I'm not saying don't socialize with people our age. In many cases, they are our lifelong friends. On the other hand, a dear friend of mine is ninety-three and just lost his wife to the awful Alzheimer's. He says he has to hang with the "young 'uns" because there is no one left. We keep trying to get him to golf with those young "whipper snapper" eighty-year-olds, so he can teach them a thing or two. He does go out to eat with what he calls his "harem" once a week. Good for him!

> "I don't talk to old people; they try to find ways to stay static. Young folks are the ones with the ideas and constantly moving forward." – Prince

2. Embrace newness and change

"Never say no to (almost) anything" is the motto of many

recent retirees. We need to keep our brains mobile and ready to learn new things, whether it is a new activity, a new language, or a new place to volunteer. The Senior Group at my church has line dancing on Monday afternoons. It's easy and fun, and you can meet new friends while moving, learning, and laughing. When the brain learns something new, the synapses learn to fire in new patterns. This keeps the brain sharp and promotes brain health. It is even suggested that brushing your teeth with your non-dominant hand or driving a new way home helps keep your brain sharp.

3. Don't consider yourself old!
Old is always ten years older than me, maybe even twenty. Many of us are living much longer than our parents and grandparents did. Mindset is a useful tool in retirement. Keeping a young mindset will keep you thinking and feeling young. It will keep you interested in meeting new people and learning more about life. Try not to walk around saying, "I'm so old." You will become what you think you are!

4. Keep moving
Have an impromptu dance party with your grandchildren, walk around the block, garden, build something new, go hiking or sailing. Do the classic walk around the mall in inclement weather. Exercise is what Ponce de Leon should have looked for when searching for the fountain of youth. The worst thing you can do for yourself is SIT. If you have a Fitbit, it beeps at you as a reminder to get up and get going, even if it's to stretch or get a drink of water. You will look and feel better if you keep moving.

5. Do something that makes you laugh and that you love.

There have been many studies that show that laughter is the best medicine. We all know people who are ill or suffering who have friends bring over funny movies. Don't wait until you are sick. Laugh now! Keep doing things that make you smile. One woman said she developed a habit, even after knee surgery, of dancing every time a Motown song came on the oldies station to which she listened. I know my childhood friend Karen still dances in the kitchen, and at the age of seventy-one, she still works twice a week as a nurse. She has severe arthritis and is beginning to get swollen joints but, I promise you, that doesn't stop her from laughing and having fun.

> "Don't act your age in retirement. Act like the inner young person you have always been."
> - J. A. West

NEW FRIENDS, NEW ACTIVITIES

Have you tried Meetups? Meetups is a gathering—a meeting—of like-minded individuals; it is international, and it is usually free. Check online at Meetups.com to find hundreds of groups near you with people who have common interests. You can try something you love to do or try something brand new to you.

Some examples of Meetup groups are:
- Social clubs
- NRG Meetup
- Comedy clubs
- After hours trail hikes
- Mahjong
- Bold Betties (an outdoor group for active women)

- Java users
- Bike clubs
- Coed soccer
- Golf associations
- Over fifty dinners groups
- Second wind hiking and camping
- Puppy socialization groups
- Mile High Horror Films
- Motorcycling
- Amateur musicians
- Mile High Nudists (Really)
- Philosophy and movies
- Metaphysics
- Gong immersion

Just about anything you could think of (or not even imagine) is available on Meetup sites. There are many ways of meeting people, learning new things, and making connections.

GRANDCHILDREN

We have an opportunity, and maybe an obligation, to teach our grandchildren about our way of life. It is an opportunity to build a lasting, loving bond and make a difference in their lives. Remember when we were working and being a parent and running in all directions? Now, if we are with our grandchildren, we can be truly present with them. Usually their own parents, our dear children, have their iPhone glued to their hand, if not their ear. We can spend time with the grands without that technology attached to us. We might be the ones to pass on spiritual values and a Biblical connection, if that is your belief.

Playing with Grands

Time with your grandchildren doesn't need to be games or a walk at the park, although that's good too! Teach your grandchild things you know how to do that they might not get to do otherwise. Show them how to do woodworking or tie a fly or play dominoes or poker. Maybe you have a magic trick and can show them how you found that quarter behind little Jason's ear. Young children like and find comfort in repetition. Having hot chocolate in their special mug or singing a favorite song when they see you become traditions

> "It is not the honor that you take with you but the heritage you leave behind."
> – Branch Rickey

and are things they remember after you are gone. If you can go to opening day of baseball season with your teenage grandson for several years, that's a fun event for you both and a lasting memory. You can think of more events like that so when they are done repeatedly, they become things you will both cherish.

Share your favorite childhood books with them; if not the book, tell the story. My granddaughter had never heard Peter Rabbit. (How

THE PLAYER

"IT IS NOT THE HONOR THAT YOU TAKE WITH YOU BUT THE HERITAGE YOU LEAVE BEHIND."
– BRANCH RICKEY

can that be?) When I told her a modified version of it, she was hooked. It is now one of our favorites to share; she has found it and enjoys it on YouTube.

If you want to go to an art museum, be sure to add pizza or ice cream afterwards. That goes for all museums and other places where we attempt to introduce something educational to the kiddos. You might come home and try your hand at duplicating the art you saw. Crayons, torn tissue paper, and watercolors are all good materials with which to have artistic experiences. It doesn't have to be oil paint, and it doesn't have to be perfect!

Your local public library is a great place to take grandchildren, from toddlers to junior high kids. Here are some events held at local libraries.

- **Story Time**
  Babies, toddlers, and preschoolers are scheduled at different days and times. These are great experiences with stories, music, and movement.
- **Bark for Books**
  Youngsters six to twelve can read to a dog for fifteen minutes.
- **Princess Party**
  All the little girls dress up and a college girl comes in her ball gown, complete with a handsome prince.
- **Lego Day**
- **Valentines and Art**
- **Chinese New Year**
  Art, food, and performances.
- **Craft Lab**

Books and art that go with the stories.

- **Sensory Story Time**
  Good for kids with special needs such as autism or hyper-sensory issues.

Hopefully these samples can help you see that your public library has a wide array of interesting and fun things for you to do with children and many times they're FREE!

There will probably come a time when you seem boring to your grandchild, usually in their "tween years." Remember at this age, their social world is expanding, and they want to be with their friends. This is a natural progression in their development. Maintain your sense of humor and try to be available when they want. Usually, if you have been close to them in younger years, they will return to value your special relationship. Maybe learn their friends' names (and try to keep them straight, Grandpa), so you can ask little Susie how her friend Ava is doing on the soccer team.

Board games, cards (do they play cards anymore?), walking the dog, and jigsaw puzzles offer a chance to be with the grandchildren without sitting face-to-face and quizzing them. Tweens and teens especially don't like that face-to-face encounter very much, especially if it involves questioning. One technique is to have a jigsaw puzzle set up in the corner. If you quietly go and sit down to play, eventually kids and grandkids will come and join in. If you don't ask them questions, they usually will begin to chat on their own. LISTEN with the occasional nod, and you can learn a lot and be another source of support in their lives at this time.

Keeping in Touch Long-Distance

If your grandchildren don't live where you can be physically, there are some fun creative ways to stay in touch.

- You can write a letter or send a surprise box of things. They will love that!
- Facetime or Skype with the grandchildren.
- Order pizza and have it sent to their house. This one is a big winner! It is especially helpful if it's on a night when Mom or Dad are running around and meal time is hectic!
- Read a story to them by Facetime or on the phone.
- Send a text message to the older ones before a concert or sporting event in which they are participating.
- Play Words with Friends or chess online, or find another online game they like to play.
- Share recipes for a once a month "dinner together." You can be on Facetime or Skype while you cook. If it's a recipe handed down from your mother or grandfather, share your memories of what those days were like.
- Have a Fantasy Football pool or another sports event. My family has a rotating trophy for an NFL football pool. We keep it simple. Each person picks two teams and gets one point for a win. At the end of the season, the trophy is mailed to the new winner, and their name is engraved on the plaque. I actually won once!" Go, Grammie!
- Create an e-mail account just for your use with each grandchild.

This account is known only to you and their parents. Write a message whenever you think of some bit of wisdom you wish to share with them or tell them a story about yourself when you were their age. This is a great way to leave your life story without sitting down and having to write your autobiography. Keep adding to it and later, it can be complied into a book or scrapbook to share. You can send pictures using this email account also.

If you choose to write your life story for them, you can do it in segments centered around events. This style removes the pressure of being a formal writer or writing the Great American Memoir. Some subjects might be:

- Christmas as a kid
- What I wore for Halloween
- My parents and me when I was eight, fourteen, and twenty-one
- School days
- Sports and me
- My first boyfriend
- My wedding day
- Raising kids
- Getting a job
- The county fair

The ideas and subjects here are endless. Let the calendar be your guide in the beginning and write how these special days—New Years, Valentine's Day, Summer Vacations, etc.—were observed in your life. If you don't want to type, use the audio recording on your computer or other device. If you don't know how to do it, ask your children, your neighbor, or even those grandkids—they'll tell you!

Add some photos of the two of you doing things together to that email account. Every few years, you can get all the emails and have them printed into a book like Shutterfly. You will be leaving them with fun stories about yourself, some words of wisdom you want them to have, and you will be creating a legacy for them. TV personality Steve Harvey says he believes it is important to leave a legacy for your grandchildren and your children's grandchildren so they will know your name. He also said he wants his progeny to know the difference between "success and greatness." This is something important for us all to think about.

Ask any pastor, priest, or rabbi. On their death bed, NO ONE ever said, "Bring me my paystubs, let me see how much I made," or, "Bring me the trophy from the club golf tournament; I want to see it again." What they do say is, "Get my family," or, "I wish I had loved and helped others more."

Put It On the Schedule

Whether you meet with family, friends, clubs, or grandchildren, put it all on the calendar, so you aren't tempted to become reclusive. We are going to have rough days. We may have aches and pains or an illness or lose loved ones and having those five friends, and maybe more, in our lives will be our safety net. Sharing both the sorrows and the good times is what gives us our humanity. Stay connected with life. It keeps us real to share the messy and the magnificent!

You Do Have Value

In addition to putting upcoming events on the schedule,

once a week or so write down the things you accomplished this week. It doesn't have to be huge things, just the things you did or places you went. Some retired folks think they have nothing to give others in terms of time or service. Some people say, "Oh, I don't have anything to do anymore; I just sit around." Making a cake to share, writing a letter, or having coffee at Denny's are all things that got you out of the house and contributed to your life. Be aware of all you do; you do have value!

The Sweet Spot

The encore, the added bonus we get to have in our lives, is in that sweet spot that begins with the initial time of our retirement and lasts fifteen to twenty years. After that, time does begin to wear on the body and mind. So use this time, your friends and family, and really rock it! Travel, try new things, go fishing—whatever it is that you've not had the time to do while you were working. Laugh, smile, enjoy it all!

"I'm not old; I'm a recycled teenager!"
- Anonymous

6
Why Are
We Here?

"Who am I?" "Why am I here?" "What is my purpose?" These are some of the questions people ask themselves as they grow from being a child to becoming a mature adult. They are the questions people ask when they are thinking there must be more to life than just going to work each day and acquiring possessions. "Am I nothing more than a plant that sprouted from a seed blown here by the wind? Am I more than that? Am I connected to a Creator? Am I connected to my fellow man?"

Because most of us, at one time or another, feel there is more to life than our day-to-day existence, it is often said that we are "hard-wired" to search for God. In many faith traditions and practices, there exist ways to connect to The Universe—to something bigger than ourselves—to God. Spirituality offers a connection or completeness as we look for more than the materialism of the world to fill an empty spot in our lives.

> "All major religious traditions carry basically the same message: that is love, compassion, and forgiveness. The important thing is they should be part of our daily lives."
> – Dalai Lama

According to Dr. Stephen Juan, writing in The Register, there were 4,300 religions in the world a decade ago. Seventy-five percent of all people practice one of the following religions. They are listed in descending order according to a 2015 PEW report.

- Christianity
- Islam
- None
- Hinduism
- Buddhism
- Judaism

Of the top six "belief systems" in the world, coming in at number three is the category "none." "None" is not a religion, rather, more often than not, it is a rejection of formalized religion and its practices. While the number of "nones" is growing, there is still the universal feeling in each of us that there is more to life than self.

More and more people, especially in the Western culture, are saying, "I'm spiritual, not religious." Most religions have a set of practices and rituals that give meaning to the believers. Different religions have different practices and rituals, but they still hold a shared belief. For example, in Christianity, the belief is that Jesus Christ was born, lived, died, and rose again for the salvation of believers. The things various denominations do in their services or observances may differ, but the basic tenets of faith are the same. In the past, Roman Catholics didn't eat meat on Fridays and Baptists, among others, did. However, both of these denominations of Christianity believe that Christ is their salvation and following His teachings is the way to eternal life.

A common theme to those who are spiritual but not necessarily religious is, "How do I live a good life? Where do I find meaning?" The connections made between the seeker and his findings bring about a sense of peace, awe, and contentment: things we all want in life.

There are also differences for those seeking to live a spiritual life. Some groups seek the connection to the Spirit or The Universe through prayer, some through meditation, some in nature. Some spiritual groups deprive themselves to the point of suffering in order to learn how to overcome it. Not all who are spiritual are in groups too. It can be a journey of understanding and connection all to one's self.

"Love the animals, love the plants, love everything. If you love everything, you will perceive the divine mystery in things. Once you perceive it, you will begin to comprehend it better every day. And you will come at last to love the whole world with an all-embracing love."
- Fyodor Dostoyevsky

In contemporary life, one who is spiritual and has a connection to a greater presence is seen as one who has a sense of holiness, attempts to be of service to others, and lives an ethical life.

As people retire and enter a time of increased reflection

on the meaning of life (when we discover—perhaps—that those "hippies from the 60s" really were doing more than just contemplating their navels), they turn to their religion or become spiritual seekers in order to answer these questions. New questions are added, for example, "How much time do I have?" and "What's next?" Richard Leider, with AARP Life Reimagined Institute says, "I believe that spirit universally touches and moves through the purposeful journey of life from cradle to grave."

With our jobs, we had a specific identity, social interaction, purpose, and —of course—we earned money and occupied our time. In retirement, not only are we looking for amusements and ways to pass the time, but we are searching, again, for meaning. Watching TV sixteen hours a day does not fill any of those roles we had as workers. Molly Srode, a retired hospital chaplain and author of *Creating a Spiritual Retirement*, has found that retirees are keenly concerned with the question of how their lives can be meaningful now that they've left behind their work and the roles they fulfilled in their jobs. They worry about aging, the changes that come with it, and what their futures hold. They're asking, "Who am I now? Am I still worthwhile? How will I handle diminishing abilities?"

> "My physical body may be less efficient and less beautiful in old age. But God has given me an enormous compensation: My mind is richer, my Soul is broader, and my wisdom is at a peak. I am so happy with the riches of my advanced peak age that, contrary to Faust, I would not wish to return to youth."
> – Robert Muller

BEING A PILGRIM

Some people attempt to answer these universal questions by taking a pilgrimage. This is an intentional, spiritual journey to deepen your faith. Some common places for pilgrimages include Muslims going to Mecca, Christians traveling to the Holy Land, and Catholics who visit Lourdes. Have you taken a pilgrimage? Did you experience a sacred awakening, a connection to a new community or new culture? Did you have a clarity of belief in your heritage or your future? Walking the Camino de Santiago in northwest Spain is such a pilgrimage. The office of Pilgrims of Santiago reports that 17.72% of those completing this pilgrimage are over sixty years of age. The number of walkers who completed it in 1986 was 2,491. In 2017, 301,036 people completed the 500-mile journey. It is obviously a popular endeavor. Perhaps you will be the next to go!

One woman who attempted that pilgrimage is a pastor from my town. She has a doctorate and a passion for music and hiking. She is widely respected by her colleagues and held positions of leadership in the church community. At sixty-six years of age, she retired. What did she do upon retirement? She certainly didn't sit and knit; she trained for a six-week hike and a deeper connection with God. She shared her story with many groups after she returned, and I was in the audience for one of her retellings. I found myself wondering, "Could I do that? I'm in shape (somewhat). Could I, would I, ever undertake such a solo endeavor?" I knew I'd be okay with the spiritual quest. The six-week hike? Not so much. Take a look at her story and wonder: Would you do this? Could you?

Reverend Janet, sixty-eight, planned on marking her retirement with a little hike: a solo walk of 500 miles and an attempt at an even closer relationship with God. Starting at Saint-Jean-Pied-De-Port, France, she planned to walk the ancient pilgrimage route across northern Spain to the Cathedral of St. James in Santiago de Compostela. Beginning in Medieval times, the Camino de Santiago path has been carved by thousands of walkers each year, walkers who visit the burial site of James, the apostle of Jesus. These pilgrims search for meaning and a closer relationship with God.

One of the things that made her journey interesting, besides being a woman hiking alone (by then at the age of sixty-eight), was the fact that just a year before, she had fallen and broken her kneecap. With a year of rehab and training, she felt ready for her quest. Jeremiah 5:16 says, "This is what the Lord says, 'Stand at the crossroads and look; ask for the ancient paths, ask where the good way is and walk in it and you will find rest for your souls.'"

At the beginning of the good way, the Camino de Santiago, Reverend Janet hoisted her backpack, grabbed her hiking poles, and said a prayer. She began her six-week journey and found that, although alone, she was not lonely. She met many fellow hikers along the way. They often found themselves at the same way station each evening. They became friends, not strangers—travelers, not tourists. Historian Daniel

Boorstein explains that in previous centuries, travelers were those interested in unfamiliar settings. Travelers sought out wild encounters to expand their perspectives. "The traveler is active, strenuously in search of people or adventure. In contrast, the tourist is passive, waiting for interesting things to happen to her. The tourist goes sightseeing."

During her second week, Rev. Janet found herself navigating slippery terrain. The trail was muddy and slick like snow. As she was coming down a hill, she began to slide. Fearful of falling and hurting her previously injured knee, she strained to stay upright and spun in circles as she slid down the hill. As a result of her attempts to protect her knee, she found the twisting and spinning had injured her ankle. Managing to get to the way station, she iced her leg and prayed for the best. The next morning, she could not walk.

The news from a local doctor was not good. "Stay off your feet for two weeks." She had saved her knee but now had a severe sprain to her ankle. Fortunately, Rev. Janet had relatives in Spain, where she went to recuperate. During her recuperation, she enjoyed not only good care but the wonderful food and culture of Spain. During her respite, she felt a need to remain true to being a traveler; she sought out ways to encounter new things and learn more of the Spanish culture. When it came time to set out again, she found she could not go on; her foot simply would not let her continue the journey.

Calling back to Colorado, she asked her husband's opinion on what she should do next. "Well," he said, "if you come home now, those places you reserved will go unused, and you will not get your money back." Janet was at first perplexed, "Did he not want me to come home? Did he care more about the money than he did about me?" Together, they decided she should go to the end point, Compostelo, and rent a place to stay for two more weeks. Now, her pilgrimage took on an unintentional turn. A pilgrimage is a perpetual moving on, venturing into the unknown and meeting fellow travelers along the way. Janet experienced the unknown in the company of strangers, the frustration of not speaking a language while needing to communicate, and she also experienced a relationship with her God. Psalm 25:3-4 says, "Show me your way, O Lord, and teach me your paths. Lead me in your truth and teach me, for you are the God of my salvation, in you have I trusted all the day long." Changes, side routes, and detours are always present in life and now; they were present in her pilgrimage. It was time to go home, but first: a visit to the end point of the path of pilgrims.

Rev. Janet attended the service at the end of the trail in the cathedral where great vessels, whose ropes are pulled on by several strong altar boys, waft their incense as a blessing over those inside.

At the beginning of her trip, Rev. Janet spent mornings in prayer and praise, asking for blessings on those she left behind. This immersion into prayer helped carry her across the terrain when the hiking was tough. It also carried her during her disappointment at not being able to walk the trail.

You may have seen pictures of scallop shells when reading about making a pilgrimage in Spain. The shells hang from the backpacks of those who travel the path. Those traveling The Camino use the scallop shell in many ways. It marks the trail, inlaid in the concrete. It can be used as a vessel for water. The scallop shell is also a metaphor, its lines representing the different routes pilgrims travel from all over the world, all walking trails that lead to one point: the tomb of Saint James in Santiago de Compostela. Just as the lines of a scallop shell originate at different points and thus have different routes, a pilgrim travels in his or her own way, still reaching the same goal at the end.

She was in a strange land, still praying, still singing praises. She sought out new encounters and struggled with a new language while staying at her rental in Spain. Rev. Janet completed her pilgrimage, but not in the way she planned. It did mark her passage from active pastor to retired, and it did give her an adventurous spiritual awakening and set her on the path for the next third of her life .

Not all pilgrimages are done by walking to famous shrines. Journeying with a loved one facing the trials of life, going on

> "The woods are lovely dark and deep. But I have promises to keep and miles to go before I sleep."
> – Robert Frost

missions, studying and building communities, and experiencing a silent retreat are all ways to experience a deeper relationship with the Lord. There is one journey, in fact, that we are all on now: we are entering the Third Age, accompanying our bodies and sometimes the mind, as they go to places unknown.

Buen Camino—have a good journey.

CREATED FOR MORE

Even if we are not on a 500-mile pilgrimage, people in the encore stage of life are often searching for more. It is now time to live in our own rhythm, go to the beat of our own drum.

Catholic writer Jack Hansen says that in his counseling with retirees, he didn't interview anyone who found the completely leisure-oriented retirement to be satisfying for the long term. "I wonder if that's because God has created us for something different than that," Hansen says. "I believe God created us for connections: connection to Him, to others, to the earth." (Hannum, Kristen. 2014. *Finding the Good Life in Retirement.*)

Along with this need for connection, Dr. Richard Johnson, a psychological clinician, counselor, and author of *Creating a Successful Retirement: Finding Peace and Purpose,* sees the need for spiritual education to increase. As we get older "the spiritual pace quickens as we experience more loss, the driving force of all human growth." All are good reasons to take the time to develop your spiritual muscle!

DIFFERENT STROKES FOR DIFFERENT FOLKS

Retirement means different things to different people. It is the phase of life in which the accumulation of "things" is no longer important. In fact, many start to give those "things" away as they downsize. We stop our working life at different ages, from late fifties to mid-seventies. Some people retire at a time when they're already ill; others experience years of vigor in their encore days. Some retire and are ready to take walking tours around the world. Others retire when their health is bad and either spend time in rehab or find more passive pursuits; still others sit and wait to die. The manner in which we retire and use our time is different. There is no right or wrong way, and our retirement can go through phases, like everything else in life. Some retirees find themselves doing things totally new to them.

Bob Lowry retired from high-pressure work in the radio industry in 2001. Since then he's involved himself in prison ministry, travel, family, and faith. He's also discovered blogging. His blog, Satisfying Retirement, has drawn more than a million views and has given him great experiences. This is something he never saw himself doing when he was younger and actively employed.

Frank and Alice set off in their late forties into what they thought might be five years of missionary work after successful careers in insurance and finance. That was seventeen years ago—years that have blossomed into a full-time second career, far from their adult children and still years from true retirement. More than a decade of those years has been spent in southeast Asia. They worked in a school and hospital setting where they took care of, fed, and taught severely dehydrated, undernourished children who were expected to die. After a few months, they saw those same children riding bicycles and laughing; this was an enormous reward for their efforts.

"We're spoiled. The people who put in wells and toilets don't get to see immediate results like that. We see the effect of our work, and it deepens our faith."

In Florida, retirees can volunteer in the Sun City Center Community Campaign Against Human Trafficking. What started with three retired women, residents of a senior center in Florida, has grown into a vigorous organization with many events and volunteers banded together to work for good. One volunteer is part of the Community Organization Team for the center. She teaches classes and speaks to community organizations, telling them about the growth of the horrendous crime of sex trafficking in their area. This volunteer says it has become a passion and admits she is not at all sorry that she's back to spending "countless hours" on this project. "But I won't do that forever," she says.

The challenge for most retirees is striking a balance, somewhere between full-time work on a volunteer basis and full days on the golf course. There needs to be time for visiting children, grandchildren, and friends, while also enjoying all the extra hours they can now call their own. It's a balance that takes thoughtfulness and effort to achieve.

"The foundations of a person are not in matter but in spirit."
- Ralph Waldo Emerson

One family that found that balance did so in a resort community in Florida. They play, they volunteer, and they grandparent, and they love it all!

My husband, Jeff, and I believe in the saying, "If you love what you do, you never work a day in your life." That was so true of my life in Scottsdale, Arizona, where I worked in retail and had my children. It was also true for Jeff, who was an investment banker on Wall Street and owned a private jet business, and other businesses, over the years.

Jeff's best friend had a home in Mirasol in Palm Beach, Florida. We often went there to visit and vacation, and we fell in love with the community. We kept staying longer and longer and decided to sell our home in Scottsdale. It sold in three days, which was good news and bad news! I had children and grandchildren in Scottsdale! We bought a townhome there, and now I come back once a month and stay a week. We also fly to New York to see our granddaughters up there.

My daily life in Mirasol begins with a water aerobics class, followed by lunch, then cards. I play canasta six days a week. There is also bridge and mah jong in the ladies' card room, which is packed every day during the "season," which runs January until May, when the winter people leave. I participate in various charities and my calendar is always full with luncheons and dinners that I or we attend.

Jeff has made many friends here too. He had been very sick with heart disease in the last few years. At one point, he needed a heart transplant. Fast forwarding the story, he got a third defibrillator, changed his meds until they got it right, lost ninety pounds, changed his eating habits, and now goes to water aerobics every morning with me. His day includes lunch with the boys and then whatever he wants to do. We meet up for dinner, and we usually go out! I still haven't used my stove or oven since I moved here. Neither he nor I miss working. Life is far too much fun, and I hope we have about thirty more years of this. I've made a ton of friends here. I've found my niche in life. Every day, I thank God for putting me here. Who's luckier than me? I've died and gone to heaven!

As we go along this path of life, different things happen to change our course. Many of us think, "I've gone to school and put in my time at work, now it's time to kick back and enjoy." For many, it is right foot, left foot, steady as she goes.

For some, an idea that was born years ago comes to bear fruit later in life. Like George in the story that follows, who earned a master's in Divinity AFTER he retired. But that wasn't all he experienced. The loss of family and friends is what gave him pause.

"When I was fully employed and raising my family, you might say I was damnably busy," says eighty-six-year-old George, who worked as a federal investigator and raised eleven children. "I was usually a mass-goer in the morning, but there were times my attention to the church was minimal." No one could describe his faith that way since he retired. After retiring at age fifty-seven and being divorced, George chose to focus on his intellectual side. He earned a master's of divinity degree from Gonzaga University in Spokane, Washington and lived in a Cistercian monastery as a porter for sixteen years. Now, still vigorous, he volunteers with the Ignatian Volunteer Corps at a senior center near Syracuse, New York.

For George, retirement has meant freedom. He thinks his transition was easy for a couple reasons. He had a firm grounding in his Catholic faith, and he could prepare for retirement; it wasn't a surprise. Divorce was his far more difficult transition. "I didn't see that coming," he says. Still, losses now tumble on top of one another. "The longer you live, the more people fall away," he says. "The people you used to talk to are no longer around." During this new phase of life, people left alone by death or divorce find that isolation becomes a new factor with which to contend. For some, it causes great depression. For others, like George, becoming an active part of a volunteer community serves two purposes. You can help others while at the same time helping yourself by developing a new network of friends. Both things are vital to those living alone.

LEAVING A LASTING LEGACY

Given a long retirement, most people realize that wealth and material possessions are not of primary importance. Generativity, the passing of knowledge from an older generation to the younger, is more valued. This can be done through modeling of our lives and sharing with grandchildren, or by serving the poor and needy, or by otherwise mentoring younger people with whom we are in contact.

Many people dread diminishing strength. We forget that aging is a natural part of the plan. Whether you are spiritual or not, the sense of our own mortality grows stronger the older we become. If a person has a faith that includes the afterlife, he realizes death is not the end of life, not the end of his existence. For him, the end is a transition to another type of existence. For those who do not have this kind of faith, there is still a sense of connection and the need to do something for others. This sense of searching for a connection or meaning is universal, not a part of organized religion. It's a desire to leave a legacy.

> "Each today, well-lived, makes yesterday a dream of happiness and each tomorrow a vision of hope. Look, therefore, to this one day, for it and it alone is life."
> – Sanskrit Poem

It is all a gift: life, retirement, work, birth, and death. It is up to us to use this time and make it an encore to be remembered!

Good luck. Now let's rock it!

7
Wrapping it Up

The First and Second Acts are over. It has been a job well done. We are being given an opportunity for more, without the constraints of a full-time job or a young family for which to care. This is the encore; how you play it is up to you!

There are many different kinds of retirements, and you know yourself and your desires. You know your values: do you want to be constantly busy, travel as much as possible, volunteer as much as you can? Do it! You have to have your health and have your finances in order; then, make it happen.

What if you are just plain tired and worn out? Perhaps you worked on the railroads or did construction all your life. Your body aches, and you want to sit. Well, you deserve your rest and relaxation. Go ahead and sit on the porch listening to the birds chirp. My father lived in the Rust Belt, and when he retired, he wanted to fish. He bought a red canoe, strapped it to the top of his car, and drove out to the lake in peace and quiet. That was his retirement fun until he died.

Much of this book has been about doing all you can and living fully. What if you find you have no energy and don't want or need to go, go, go all the time? Karen's story demonstrates that we don't have to be productive every day.

I was a stay-at-home mom until I divorced in my early forties. I did some different things, including returning to school and getting a master's in counseling when I was fifty. I worked as a counselor both as an intern before getting my license and then in private practice for about fifteen years. While I was in school and in-between counseling positions, I worked in administration as a clerical associate.

When I moved to the Denver area thirteen years ago, after living in Southern California for over thirty years, I didn't want to jump back into the responsibility of counseling, but I did want to do something where I felt helpful. I cared for seniors for a year or so until my daughter sent me an email that Anchor Center for Blind Children was looking for a part-time office manager. I applied and joined Anchor Center in July of 2006. Initially I worked two days a week, but shortly went to three days a week. I worked for Anchor Center about seven years.

In the beginning with Anchor Center, I had a flexible schedule that allowed me to work two days in a row and then later three days in a row. However, at some point, I realized I needed time in-between my working days to sleep more and "recover." The staff and my co-workers at Anchor Center were okay with intermittent days off, and I was able to continue that way until I retired five years ago, just shy of seventy-four years of age. The Anchor Center position was super: I was in a caring organization where I felt helpful; I enjoyed the clerical work and interacting with staff, families, and the public; and I got to know many wonderful Delta Gamma sorority sisters who were very involved with Anchor Center. Perfect!

I'm not sure when it was I became aware that I needed more sleep than I got in my younger days. In 2009, when I met with college friends, I knew I needed a room of my own. As we have continued to get together since then, they sometimes started the day without me and I would "catch up" with them later on. Sometimes, I needed to take a day or part of the day off during our four-day reunions because I got too tired. During my last several months at Anchor Center, I realized I was feeling physically tired and that I needed more and more sleep. When I take road trips, I bring food with me, so I can have breakfast in the room and not start out until noon or later. Hotel/motel breakfasts that end at nine or ten a.m. are too early for me. Early in my retirement, I needed ten hours sleep nightly. Now it's closer to twelve.

Since my retirement five years ago, I have, until very recently, continued to feel I needed to always be productive: clean the house, pay the bills, balance the checkbook, wash the clothes, walk the dog, exercise, socialize, answer the phone, etc.! I have known for some time that I really enjoyed the days I didn't have anything "scheduled." Those days gave me time to do all those productive things. When I left the house, it broke my concentration, and I didn't get back to the things I wanted to do. A few months ago, I decided to start putting "nothing scheduled" (NS) on free days on my calendar. After a few weeks of really enjoying those days, I started scheduling them, rather than just waiting for them to show up. I also began grouping appointments on the same day so I could set aside more NS days. As I had more time for me (and more sleep because I don't set an alarm on my NS days), I realized that I didn't have to be productive all the time when I was home. I could read, play with the dog, hold the dog on my lap, and enjoy my digital scrapbooking. With unscheduled days, I can get the house clean and the bills paid, etc. I just get them done in a more re-laxed way. I can be productive, but I don't **have** to be. It's new for me, so tension does show up sometimes. However, I am also more in the present and experienc-ing more peace. What a concept!

The study of positive psychology tells us we do our best when we live well with ourselves and others. We need relationships, kindness, exercise, health, a positive mindset—all those things we've discussed in this book. Openness to trying new things and resiliency to changes are also important. Our minds are wired to keep us in safety zones, otherwise known as "a rut." When we consider trying something new, little alarms go off saying "maybe not; maybe you shouldn't; we haven't done this before!" If we wait too long, the adage, "He who hesitates is lost" comes into play. This is interesting because, on one hand, we do want to be safe but, on the other hand, new adventures await—and they keep the mind sharp. So, my advice, go for it! Whether it's a new Indian place for dinner or a new state you haven't see or a new sport, try it!

If you are feeling unmotivated, do it anyway. We need energy to get things done, **and** getting things done gives you more energy, **and**, you feel better about yourself, **and** then you get motivated to get more things done. (See how this goes here, like a hamster wheel!)

Life at this stage of retirement goes by quickly and changes will occur. This is when resiliency will play an important role, as well as a good sense of humor and a positive outlook. When a sudden and possibly life-altering change, such as a major illness, occurs, we need to be able to adapt, adjust, and accept things. This might be a good time to take up scrapbooking or find a cause that needs your skills of writing letters to editors.

What if you are alone by choice, divorce, or death; what then? Living alone doesn't have to mean lonely. I started my retirement after my twenty-five year marriage ended. My finances were in order and so was my health. Needing to be on a new trajectory, I moved to a new city. Three of my four adult children lived in Denver, and I was already familiar with the city and knew where I wanted to get a condo. I made new friends in my neighborhood, church, and gym. Because of connections I made with an international non-profit, I went to Africa three times and am planning another trip now.

Civic, churches, and health organizations are becoming more and more aware of the issue of isolation and are making attempts at offering ways for people to make connections. Be sure to look for opportunities at places you go, from local libraries, to health centers, nearby recreation centers, and churches or synagogues.

THE BIG FINISH

Ask yourself these questions and use the space for your answers:

If I had all the money I needed, how would I live?

_____

_____

_____

If I were going to live forever, what would I do?

_____

_____

_____

If I were going to die in a month, what would I do?

_____

_____

_____

If I were afraid of nothing, what would I do?

_____

_____

_____

Who do I admire? _____

_____

_____

What do I value? _____

_____

_____

Look at your answers to these questions and then ask yourself, "What is stopping me from doing these things? Or how could I make this possible?" This is it; this is your time, and there is not going to be a do-over. See the parts of the world you always wanted to see. Create those memories with your spouse or your grandchildren. Make sure you've given it all you've got; you can't take it with you!

> "Life should not be a journey to the grave with the intention of arriving safely in a pretty and well-preserved body, but rather to skid in broadside in a cloud of smoke, thoroughly used up, totally worn out, and loudly proclaiming, 'Wow! What a Ride!'"
> – Hunter S. Thompson

If you find yourself stuck and unable to figure out how to keep the juices flowing in retirement, you can find my contact information at the back of this book. Get in touch, and let's see what we can do together to give you a rockin' encore. Until then, you ARE a Rockstar; go take that bow!

Acknowledgments

I must first pay tribute to my parents, Velma and Ralph Myrick. They instilled in me all the areas that are mentioned in this book. I was a lover of reading and education; they saw to it that I had every lesson known to man, even once having a man with an accordion come to teach me (that didn't fly, not even one minute). I was gregarious and learned early on that there was a good time to be had, and it was up to me to have it. I often took walks with my mother and we had deep, spiritual conversations. Although not well-off financially, they taught me to save money while still taking every opportunity to travel. Thanks, Mom and Dad.

To the Denver Chapter of the National Speakers

Association, for that's where I was introduced to My Word Publishing and many other fantastic groups and individuals. It was there that I fine-tuned the craft of public speaking that I had begun at Toastmasters International.

To Polly Letofsky and the team at My Word Publishing: You all are amazing; you gently, yet firmly, prodded me along, and I finally having a book worthy of the reader. Special recognition to Polly Letofsky, Andrea Costantine, Victoria Wolf.

To Bobby Haas, my editor. I have always seen authors write tributes to "my editor without whom this book would not be what it is." I truly understand that now. I have written and had published five other books, biographies for children. THAT was a piece of cake. THIS was long and arduous, yet my editor kept asking for "more here, stronger there; this part is a little tired. What do you mean by this?"

THANK YOU to Bobby for making this book so much more than what I first sent to you. You said I would come to hate you; it hasn't happened. Thank you!

Finally, to my family, friends, and colleagues who had to hear, "My book, my book. Listen to what I learned today," when researching isolation, health, fitness, religion, AARP, or whatever else I was pursuing. Your patience and feedback have been invaluable. I appreciate you all.

About the Author

Marilyn Myrick Watson is the recipient of The Arizona Centennial Legacy Project designation for her contribution to the state's centennial by writing five biographies for children. Her biographies of famous Arizonans include Barry Goldwater, Rose Mofford (the first female governor in Arizona), Raul Castro (the first Hispanic governor), Frank Luke, Jr., and Poston and Hunt: Arizona's Founding Fathers. She was also nominated as Phoenix Woman of the Year for this project.

Born in Steubenville, Ohio, she is the daughter of an avid reader. She received a BS in education and library science from Miami University. After moving to Arizona, Watson earned her MA in counselor education. After teaching in the classroom for four years and serving in the district office for three, Marilyn became the school librarian: a position she lovingly held for twenty-five years. She is the proud mother of four grown children and nine grandchildren.

She has been involved in developing libraries overseas. Her first international library work was on an island in Lake Titicaca, Peru, with the Paradise Valley Reading Council. Later, she was involved with a small NGO in Kenya, bringing libraries to rural areas. She still returns to do in-service classes for teachers , helping them learn to utilize the libraries more.

In her spare time, she volunteers teaching a class on purpose and potential to those seeking to climb out of poverty and despair, and does other community volunteer work.

While living in Germany for two years, she acquired a love of traveling, and her suitcase is packed and ready. She is a speaker and life coach for those in transition. You may contact her for personal coaching or speaking to audiences both large and small. Marilyn will also come to book clubs in person in the Denver area or by Zoom or Facetime

www.marilynmyrickwatson.com

www.Encorethebook.com

marilynmwat@gmail.com

You can also follow Marilyn on Facebook at Encore! A Boomer's Guide to a Rocking Your Retirement.

If you enjoyed this book, please consider leaving a review on Amazon or your favorite book review site. Spread the word so we can Rock This Retirement!

Made in the USA
Las Vegas, NV
20 January 2021